C-A-T = (

TEACH YOUR CHILD TO READ
WITH PHONICS

In the same series

Brush Up Your Grammar
The Right Way To Spell

Uniform with this book

C - A - T
=
CAT

TEACH YOUR CHILD TO
READ WITH PHONICS

Mona McNee

RIGHT WAY

Typeset in 11pt Times by Letterpart Ltd., Reigate, Surrey.

Printed and bound in Great Britain by Cox & Wyman Ltd., Reading, Berkshire.

The *Right Way* series is published by Elliot Right Way Books, Brighton Road, Lower Kingswood, Tadworth, Surrey, KT20 6TD, U.K. For information about our company and the other books we publish, visit our web site at www.right-way.co.uk

CONTENTS

STEPS		PAGE
	Introduction	7
1-3	c a t	14
4-6	d o g	18
7-8	f x	20
9-10	v n	22
11-13	z i p	24
14-15	w, e	26
16	r	27
17	m	28
18-19	j u	29
20	l	31
21-23	h k b	32
24	s	37
25	y	39
26	q	41
27-30	Four-letter words	56
31-35	Longer words	61
36-37	oo ee	70
38	sh	73
39	ch	74
40	th	75
41	ar	80
42	or	82
43-45	er ir ur	87

46-50	-e	94
51	Doubling	104
52-54	-le	108
55	oa	114
56-60	i, y; ai, ay; oi, oy	115
61-62	ea	126
63-68	Soft c, g	132
69	gu	150
70-71	ou	151
72-73	ow	153
74-75	au aw	157
76-77	gh ght	159
78	ought	160
79-88	-ough	161
89	wa	164
90	wh and short words	165
91	al wor	166
92	Words of French origin	169
93	The long sound of u	170
94	Words of Greek origin	171
95	Silent letters	175
96	Silent h, g	176
97	-tion	177
98	-ture	179
99	ie	180
100	be- re- de-	181
Games		183

INTRODUCTION

You *can* teach your own child to read. You do not need special training, just common sense and the will to *teach* (not to help, encourage, or facilitate, but specifically to *teach*) reading bit by bit, and not to allow *guessing* to play any part.

Teaching children, or adults, to read is simple and does not take long. You just need a structured phonic programme. You start at the beginning with letters and sounds. The pupil learns how to sound out, how to blend three sounds in a word, how to make **c-a-t** into **cat**. This early blending is most important. Then he moves on to longer words. When the pupil can read words like **comic** and **hundred**, he has completed the first third of learning to read. At this stage he *knows* that he can get the word from the letters (not from an accompanying picture); he does not need someone else to tell him what the words are. Both tutor and learner know exactly where they are up to and what the next task is. There is fun in the games described in the programme, but the main incentive is success. It is exciting.

This programme is called *phonics* (not phonetics which uses a different set of symbols). Instead of learning how to 'recognise' whole words first, the pupil learns the bits and how to put them together.

The second third of learning to read is to learn those

sounds for which we use two or more letters: **sh** as in
fish; **aw** as in **crawl**, and so on. The final third is gaining
fluency, and it is at this point that great benefit arises
from reading, and practice. By this time, an element of
self-tutoring has developed.

Reading to and with children is a pleasant family activity, but it is not the same thing as teaching them *how* to
read. Teaching reading starts with phonics. Many children
just cannot start on whole words and whole books. Phonics gives them a chance. It does not confuse, it harms
no-one and even for those children who can read before
they start school, phonics-first will improve their spelling.

Starting this simple way, with letters and sounds, children are ready by their fourth birthday if not before.
Children should learn to read in their first school year,
either nursery or reception class. It is only when reading is
taught using the 'whole-word' method that teachers think
children are 'not ready', that learning to read takes years
and years, and that children who are dyslexic develop
problems needlessly. Phonics rescues dyslexics.

Before you begin
Read each day's programme through before you start, the
day before, to make sure you have all the materials you
need.

Make a note of the date you begin using the programme
so that, when you reach the end, you'll know how long it
took.

Praise
This book gives you ideas and a programme, but use your
own ideas too. Throughout the whole programme, both
you and the pupil should be enjoying yourselves. Pour out
the praise endlessly.

If the pupil gets stuck or makes a mistake, avoid saying,
'No' or 'That's wrong'. See if any of it is right. Say,
instead, 'Let's try again', 'Have another look' or, perhaps,

'Slow down'. Later on, in spelling, say, 'You have got six letters right, in the right order, and now you need just one more letter to get it right. *Listen* to the word again ... Now – where have you lost a sound? Where would you need to add a letter in your spelling? Which sound, which letter?' Comment on all the things that are right; do not praise without justification, but find *something* to praise. If it is 'just one of those days', laugh and say, 'Well, tomorrow is another day'.

Length of lessons
Aim at about 30 minutes a day, but this is not rigid. A school could use the full 60 minutes of the Literacy Hour for class teaching, for one or two terms of Reception Year. Use your judgment. Some good days may allow an hour, other days just ten minutes, but try to do a bit each day, even if it is only playing a game. Varied activity extends the span of attention, and thereby the lesson: games, handwriting, spelling, reading rules, hangman, anagrams, stories, etc., all make it interesting.

Give the pupil as much time as he needs to puzzle out a word. (For convenience, I use 'he' for the pupil and 'she' for the tutor, but I have known some excellent father teachers.) For some children some steps may be slow. If you can see that there is a block, tell the child the word and go on, but telling the word is a last resort, a very rare event. We are trying to convince the pupil that *he* can read the words! Telling a word implies as well that adults (readers) read words and not the learner. Telling a word may also give the impression that reading must be fast. In the end it will be, but someone learning how to read needs time. There is no hurry.

Forming the letters
We read from print, which is made up of letters, so the first task is to learn the 26 letters, how to write each one on a line, and its sound.

The dot-to-dot examples I include in this book show how the letters should be formed. On these, the dots show where there should be a flowing line, not a slow dot-by-dot join. Where there are dashes you go there-and-back, in two directions.

Teach at least a letter a day, perhaps up to four letters a day. It does not matter what letters you start with, so long as you leave **b** until near the end, and **y** and **q** (in that order) until the very end. I begin with **cat** and **dog** because they include five of the six letters that start with a backward arc.

Using letter cards
You need to make a large card (40cm × 30cm/15" × 12"), with the alphabet written in lower case in large black letters in two straight lines (**a-m**, **n-z**).

a	b	c	d	e	f	g	h	i	j	k	l	m
n	o	p	q	r	s	t	u	v	w	x	y	z

Some people prefer to arrange the letters in an arch like a rainbow, with **a** bottom-left, **m** at the top and **z** bottom-right. I also underline the vowels in red.

Then you need a smaller card with the following letters written large in two rows:

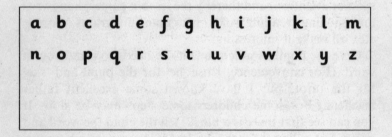

i	g	c	w	l	x
m	s	f	o	e	d

Finally, you need 26 small cards, about 2.5cm/1" square, with one letter written on each. I put the lower case on one side, and the capital on the other in a different colour. (I teach capital letters as they crop up.) You will need extra small cards for commonly used letters: **a**, **c**, **e**, **s**, etc – you will soon realise which they are. The examples given on pages 189 and 190 will guide you.

The first step is to give the pupil one of the small individual cards and see if he can find that shape on the card which shows 12 letters. Give him a **w**, then an **s**, an **x**, an **i**, and so on. If he can do this, and he is talking, he is ready to start learning to read. If he is three and not talking, teaching him to read by this method is a form of speech therapy and can help him to learn to talk at the same time. The programme can also correct speech in order to improve spelling, saying *think* instead of *fink*, for instance. The sooner children start, the better. By school age, all children are ready, if you start with letters and sounds.

At first, you will give the pupil just one letter at a time to match up by its shape. Then, as he gets better at this, you can give him all the twelve letters for the first card. When he can do this easily, you can let him match them up on the big alphabet-card. Seeing the 26 letters shows him that learning the letters is finite; he can see how many he has to learn altogether. One boy learning sight words asked his mother how many words there were, and when she replied, 'Oh, I don't know – thousands!', he gave up.

You can use these letters and the big card all through the programme. At some point, the pupil will learn the alphabet by singing it, but you will be surprised how quickly he learns the place for each letter. Indeed, most people are surprised how quickly someone, especially a child, can learn anything, once you *teach* him instead of hoping he will catch on just from being surrounded with materials and encouraged.

Using the small letters is a painless way to improve spelling. The pupil can pick out letters for sounds he can hear, and instead of you putting red ink on his written mistakes, you just have to re-arrange the letters (or let him re-arrange them), or take out the wrong letters, or leave a space for a missing letter. He then has to *listen* to the word and *hear* how the spoken word does not match the letters he has chosen and to *hear* what letters he needs to provide the missing sounds.

We read with our ears.
We spell with our ears.

Learning to listen

At the same time as the pupil is learning that letters have sounds and shapes that are written in a particular way, that they sit on lines, and how to hold a pencil, he is also going to learn the very valuable skill – a trick, really – of blending sounds into words (phonemic awareness).

On small cards the size of playing cards, write a three-letter word on one side and stick or draw a picture on the other. Show the pupil the word, point to each letter and sound it, and make sure the child is *listening*. It is a good idea to start with letters that can continue, like **fffooooox** or **Ssssaaaammm**, so that you can continue the sounds without a break while you point to the letters. For the first two or three, the child may not grasp what he is supposed to do, and you will have to show him that, when you sound **fffooooox**, there is a picture on the reverse of a fox. Then you can introduce words like **cat** where the **c** is a sharp sound, and extending it would be artificial like stuttering.

So this programme is multi-sensory: while the pupil is looking at the letter with his eyes, he will sound it with his voice and thus hear it with his ears, and write it or go over it with his fingers using his muscles. This helps to prevent fidgeting, and helps concentration. By using all his senses (except smell and taste!) you never need to worry about his strengths and weaknesses.

Which letters to teach first

I do not teach **a**, then **b**, then **cde** because this makes **b** and **d** very close together. I present first (in **cat**, **dog**) five letters that are written with the same starting action as **c** (**c**, **a**, **d**, **o**, **g**). If you get **d** well learned, starting with up-and-back-round . . ., and leave **b** nearly to the end, teaching it with the 'l' letters (**h**, **k**), you prevent **b/d** confusion. Make sure you leave **q** to the end because there is no simple three-letter word with a **q**.

How long will it take?

This programme is set out in steps, but this is only a guide. While some children will go through it much faster than others, older children will not need to spend much time on the letters. Just make sure that they do know their 26 letters and the **kw** sounds for **qu**, that they get **b/d** right, **p/q** and **y**. Adults may use this programme to brush up their spelling; they just go through it quickly until they come to some part where they hesitate. That is where they begin. But in general, both for infants just learning and adults with problems, we do need to raise expectations both for achievement and speed of learning. All children should learn to read, write and spell regular and common words in two years or less.

Ready at their fourth birthday, children should be reading by their sixth birthday. For children older than six, parents should not accept the advice, 'Don't worry. He'll catch on. It's early days yet'. It is the early learning that gives the automaticity we need when we read. And, world-wide, millions have failed to learn to read for lack of early, systematic, simple phonics.

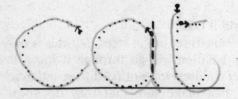

STEPS 1, 2 AND 3

c a t

Sit at a table with your child. You have probably already read a story to him, and he knows that you can look at print and say words. We do not need to labour this. Use the headlines of a newspaper to show that there are single letters – 'This is a letter, and this, and this . . .' – and that they are grouped together in what we call words, with spaces in between so that you can see where one word ends and the next begins.

On a sheet of paper, draw two lines about 3cm/1" apart: one to write on and the other to show the height of the small letters. If you have a blackboard, draw two lines 15cm/6" apart.

Direction

We read letters and words from left to right, and line by line, from top to bottom of the page. Does the child know what 'top' and 'bottom' mean?

If he has not learned left and right, put a marker of some kind (a picture of something attached with a paper clip perhaps) on the left side of the paper or put a toy like a teddy bear up on the wall to the left of the blackboard, and say, 'You start at this side at Teddy and go this way'. Hold the child's hand as he points, to move it from left to right to get the feel of the direction. If this left-right direction is explained at the start, and a finger points out the letters or words as you work, it is usually no trouble. Prevention of confusion with **saw/was**, **of/for/from** depends on what you do *at the beginning*: the left-right direction becomes automatic.

How letters are formed

Show how letters are made up of straight lines (**l**, **x**, **v**, **w**, **z**) and parts of a circle (**o**, **c**, **s**) and combinations of both. An **s** is most of a circle drawn backwards and then most of another circle going the other way. You can take letters to pieces: an **h** is a straight line down then up, a semi-circle over the top and then straight down to the line; and so on.

Using the 12-letter card and the small individual cards you prepared earlier (see page 10), show the child one of the individual cards and ask him to point out which is the same letter on the larger card. If you have a blackboard and are teaching a class of children, draw the 12-letter grid on there instead.

Holding the pencil

Before the pupil starts to write, make sure he has the correct pencil grip the *first time* he holds a crayon or pencil. The thumb and side of the long (middle) finger do the gripping, with the index finger sitting loosely on top. *Prevent* bad habits. If pencil grip is a problem, you can get a good, cheap plastic, triangular pencil-grip from educational suppliers. Left-handed writers will probably need to have their paper more slanted (left side higher) than right-handed people, who are comfortable with "straight" paper, or paper slightly slanted up on the right side.

Start with c-a-t

Explain to the pupil that you can have a real, live cat, you have the spoken word **cat** and by a wonderful invention – letters – we can write **cat** on paper.

To start with **cat**, show how you draw back-up to the top line, then keep going round to the bottom line and then up a bit, making about three-quarters of a circle. Show on a round clock how **c** starts not at the top, not at 12 o'clock, but at 2 o'clock, and goes *back-up* and round to 6 and up to 4. Get the child to 'draw a **c** in the air', swinging his arms from the shoulder and get him to say '**kuh**'. Ideally we would try to sound the '**k**' sound without the '**uh**' bit, but it is not easy, and the extra sound does not bother most people.

For the **a**, say, 'We start with a **c**, the same movement again, but this time we keep going, right round and then straight up to the top guide-line and down to the bottom line: and this is an **a**.' Get the pupil to draw it in the air, saying '**a**', the short vowel sound as in **cat**. For the **t**, point out that there are two beginnings: first a downward one, then a left-right one. Show that the cross on the **t** goes along the top guide-line. The cross-bar in some fonts starts at the vertical as shown on the dot-to-dot example at the start of the chapter or sometimes goes right across as in **t**. With two guide-lines, the tall letters (except **d**) start above the top line, and the 'tails' go below the bottom line. Using the dot-to-dot example at the start of the chapter, show how the letter starts at the big black dot, goes the way the arrow points (and explain how arrows work), along the dots, and when the dots change to dashes the line goes there-and-back. If there is only one arrow, the whole letter is completed before lifting the pencil from the page, as in **c** and **a**, but **t** has two starts.

The picture of the cat above the dot-to-dot example is not part of some fascinating story. The fascination is in learning to make letters talk. The picture is only there in case the learner forgets the three letters, and can then remind himself from the picture and not by asking the teacher. Pupils must ask us to explain what they do not understand, but we want to make them as independent as we can, from the start.

Let the pupil go over each letter many times, with his finger, with a pale-coloured crayon or felt pen, then with a darker pen. Let him practise on scrap paper. He must go over a letter, look at it, sound it, *hear* it, all at the same time. He must learn the sound of '**kuh**' as in **cat**. If you wish him to learn the name and the sound as '**Cee** says **kuh**', you can. In the end he will have to know both name and sound, but at the beginning it is the sounds that are essential. He must be able to *hear* the sounds and join them together to make the word.

Pick out the letters from the large alphabet card (see page 10) and then show how you put them back into their place. You can do this for all the letters as they are learned.

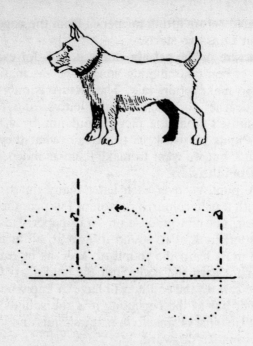

STEPS 4, 5 AND 6

d o g

Teach the letter **o**, then show how from four letters **c a t o** we can also make **a**, **at**, **act**, **cot**. If **act** is a new word, explain it.

Teach the letters **d** and **g** and get the pupil to write the word **dog**. Get him to write the letters, large, in the air, saying the sounds at the same time. Show that **d** starts with a **c** and it is the only letter where we draw *up* to the tall part, and do not start with a down movement.

Get him to write **cat**, **cot**, **dot**, **tag**, **got**, **at**, using the two guide-lines. Remind him that the letters sit on the bottom line; the small letters fit exactly and the tall letters either start above or, for a **d**, go up above the top line.

cat cot dot tag got at

Set out the large alphabet card. Select from the individual letter cards the six letters you have taught so far and put these six cards on top of their own particular letter on the large alphabet card. This shows the pupil that he has learnt six letters. Let the pupil pick out the letters to make **tag**, **cog**, **dog**, **dot**, **got**, **god**, so that he can see he is learning how letters work, the left-right direction, and where letters belong in the alphabet. Show that knowing only six letters, we can read ten or eleven words.

Play the Dice Game, Pairs and use 'Is it?' books (see the section on Games, page 183), letting the pupil sound the letters he knows, and you sound the others, but let the pupil be the one to say the complete word. Always let him take as much time as he needs: it is better to be right slowly than wrong fast. Speed has no virtue at this stage; it develops of its own accord as the pupil learns more; trying for speed usually ends up with the pupil guessing and making mistakes.

STEPS 7 AND 8

ƒ x

Teach the letters **ƒ** and **x**. **ƒ** begins with the top of a circle, and we go 'back up, over, round and down', not down-up like an **r**. Show how you can build: **fat**, **fad**, **fog**, **cox** (the one who calls the stroke in the Boat Race).

X: Sometimes children find it hard to make the parts of an **x**, **z** and **k** slope down properly. Practising with a box will help this. Show how the **x** fits into a square box.

If a pupil forgets a letter, go back to where he learned it, let him sound out the three letters and *remind himself* what the letter says. If the letter he wants is at the end of **dog**, then it says the last sound in **dog**.

If you teach '**A** for **apple**' or '**Annie apple**', your pupil(s) can end up thinking '**A** says **apple**' and giving too much importance to the first letter. This is why I use only a few words in which they can learn the letters, with all the letters *equally important*; they get the left-right direction and hearing-sounds-in-words all the time, non-stop.

Clear speech helps spelling. **F** is said by biting the bottom lip. This must be clearly fixed to the letter **f**, so that when **th** is introduced it is *not* **f**.

X is the only letter that makes two sounds: '**ks**' or, voiced, **gz**.

Say other words like **box**, **fox**, **fix**, **mix**, **six**, **next**, **exact**, **exit**, **expand**, and **expect**, and explain them if necessary, so that the pupil can hear the **x** sounds.

STEPS 9 AND 10

v n

Set out the large alphabet card and the eight small letter-cards for the letters already learned. Revise their sounds. Then move on to **v** and **n**. **V** is the shape of a valley. Find a picture of a valley and explain what it is. We go up a mountain and down the other side, and the point is at the top. Between two mountains, you go down to the river at the bottom, down into a valley, and up the next mountain. A valley is, in a way, the opposite of a mountain, and has the point at the bottom. The point should *be* a point, and not a curve. The **v** is made of two straight lines, down-up.

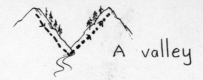

A valley

Show how knowing two more letters gives access to more words: **can**, **nag**, **not**, **fan**, **tan**, **and**, **van**, **ant**. Let the learner build up those words by picking out the right letters as you say each word, and then replacing them in the alphabet.

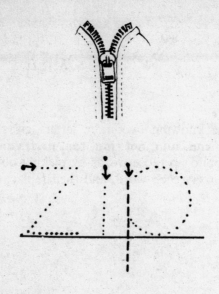

STEPS 11, 12 AND 13

z i p

As mentioned when teaching the letter **x**, sometimes children find it hard to make the parts of a **z** slope down properly. Show how **z** fits into a square box.

Draw the **i** with the downstroke first, and then the dot.
Draw the **p** as 'down-up-and-round', with the bubble sitting on the line.

Add the three letters to the known alphabet, and let the pupil make up new words by listening to sounds: **tip**, **dig**, **fig**, **pig**, **cap**, **zap**, **pod** (as in **pea-pod**), **pat**, **pot**, **top**, **fit**, **pit**, **fizz** – if you have a (consonant) sound twice, you only sound it once.

Play Pairs and the Dice Game (page 183 and page 185), letting the pupil sound out more and more letters each day.

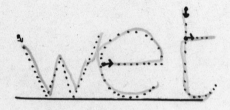

STEPS 14 AND 15

w, e

Teach the letters **w** and **e**.

A **w** is rather like two **v's**, and the French call it 'double **v'**. You can see lots of **w** on the pavement, where the lid of the water-stop-cock is marked **WATER**. Set out the alphabet card, and add **w** and **e**, making 15 letters now learnt – past halfway.

Make new words: **net, vet, get, pet, den, ten**.

STEP 16

r

Teach the letter **r**. This starts at the top, and is down-up-and-over. It does not start on the line at the bottom. It has the same movement as an **n** but stops short.

Make new words: **rip, rod, rid, ran, rot**.

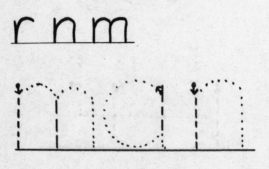

r n m

STEP 17

m

Teach the letter **m**. Show how **m**, **n** and **r** all start with the same down-up. Sound **m** with the lips closed, humming, not '**mer**'. ('**Mer**' has two sounds.)

Make new words: **mat**, **ram**, **dam**, **dim**, **mop**, **map**.

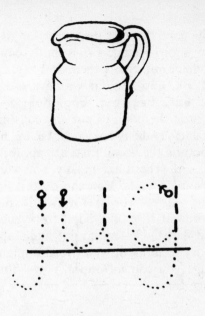

STEPS 18 AND 19

j u

Teach the letters **j** and **u**. Sound the sounds, not the names. For a **u**, say 'U (with a short sound as in **gun**) goes **u**nder and **u**p'.

Make new words: **rug**, **mug**, **cup**, **puff**, **dug**, **up**, **pup**. Get the pupil to read *and spell* these words.

A short **u** sometimes has a slightly different, deeper sound, as in **put**, **bull**, **pull**.

For **j**, make these new words: **jet**, **jot**, **jam**, **jog**.

Sing the alphabet. The best tune to use is that used for the nursery rhyme *Mary had a little lamb*. Touch each letter as you sing it.

Vowels

You have now gone through the letters for all five vowels,
sounding the short sound. (**Y** is both consonant and
vowel.) Pick them out. Show them and say, 'Their names
are **ay**, **ee**, **I**, **oh**, **you**'. So far we have used their short
sound as in: **bag**, **beg**, **big**, **bog**, **bug**. Some reading
programmes train the pupil to put any consonant in front
of the vowels and say the two sounds: **ba**, **be**, **bi**, **bo**, **bu**; or
the reverse, putting the vowel first: **ab**, **eb**, **ib**, **ob**, **ub**, **am**,
em, **im**, **om**, **um**. These are mostly not words, but are
practice in joining sounds. You can do this if you wish. I
prefer to sound out real words. However, if you do practise
using non-words, it stops the pupil from guessing: if the
learner is told that the letters do not make up a word, he
will then not try to think of what word it might be.

At this stage you can introduce Vowel Puzzles to the
pupil. See page 188.

STEP 20

l

Teach the letter **l** – a long line. (See overleaf for the dot-to-dot picture.) Make new words: **let, lit, lot, lap, log, leg, lag, lad, pull, pal, pill, doll, tell**.

Point out that the **l** at the end of a word should sound the same as the **l** at the beginning. In words like **well, tell, apple**, the **l** should *not* say '**oo**'. **Apple** is *not* '**appoo**'. The tongue should be up behind the top teeth, and *the lips should not come forward*. If the pupil is saying '**we-oo**' for **well**', use a mirror and let him see that he is not saying a **l**.

Let the pupil reach high into the air and then come down to drawn an **l**: **l** is a long line.

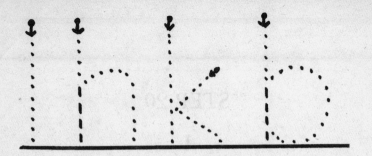

STEPS 21, 22 AND 23

h k b

Teach the letters that start with an **l**: **h**, **k**, **b**. After writing the **l**, you can only add on a bit further along the line. You cannot come down to write an **l** and then go backwards to make a **d**. A **k** has two (not three) starts: down-off, then in-out-off. As mentioned when introducing **x**, sometimes children have trouble with writing a **k**. If so, get them to practise writing it using a box for guidance.

Explain that sometimes two letters (**ck**) make one sound. Show that the name **Jack** has a different kind of **j**, a capital **J**, and that it has a line across the top instead of a dot, and it stands on the line. Explain that we call all the big letters capitals, and we use them at the beginning of names of people, countries, rivers, days, months, etc., and at the beginning of a sentence. Teach capital letters as they crop up, one at a time. They are all tall, with no tails, so nothing goes below the line.

A B C D E F G H I J K L M N O P Q R S T U V W X Y Z

We use 'sentences' when we say things like the following:
   'We are hungry.'
   'It is raining.'
Letters make words, words make sentences, and sentences make stories.

When **k** is at the end of a short, one-syllable word with a short vowel, we must put a **c** in front of it, as in **Jack** and in the following words. Get the pupil to practise writing these:

pack	**peck**	**pick**
rack	**deck**	**tick**
back	**neck**	**lick**
hack		**kick**
tack		**nick**

lock	**duck**
rock	**buck** (bucking bronco and slang for a dollar)
mock	**puck** (used in ice hockey)
dock	**luck**
	suck

Teach **b**: *bat and a ball*.

For older children and adults who have confused **b**/**d**, you show that they are *not* the same. Only one starts at the top, the **b**. You draw a straight line down (a bat) and on the right of it you draw the ball, so that the **bat** can hit the **ball** along the empty line (to write) or along the line the way we read (to read). The pupil must think: 'b**at** and b**all** – **b**'. If he notices that the **a** of **ball** doesn't have the short 'a' sound of **cat**, tell him that you'll be covering that sound later (in Step 91).

The letter **d** is different. It starts with a **c** and it is the only letter where we draw *up* to the tall part, and do not start with a down movement. Ask if the child knows **a**, **b**, **c**, **d**. If he does, show him how to tap out the **a**, **b**, with his non-writing hand, and then draw the **c** and keep going to make a **d**. To get a **d** right, he must say to himself: **a**, **b**, <u>**c**</u>, **d**.

Anagrams

Get the pupil to unjumble the anagrams on the following pages.

Anagrams (jumbled words)

j u g
_____

v a n r
_____

c o t
_____

Anagrams (jumbled words)

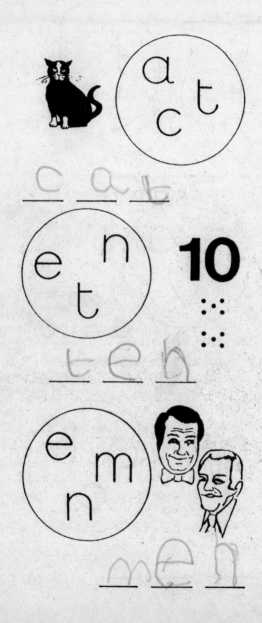

_c_ _a_ _t_

_t_ _e_ _n_

_m_ _e_ _n_

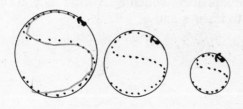

STEP 24

s

Teach the letter **s**. It fits inside a circle. The top bend of the **s** should be, if anything, smaller, tighter, than the bottom bend. We can say that the **s** is the shape of a snake, and it makes the same sound. Do snakes hiss? I have never heard one! Make new words, to read and spell: **sat**, **set**, **sun**, **sum**, **sip**, **sad**, **sag**, **gas**, **sick**, **sock**, **suck**, **ask**.

Some people pronounce the **a** in **cat** and **ask** in the same way. If the regional custom is to say '**ahsk**', then say to the pupil, 'It looks like **ask** and we say **ahsk**.' Give this reminder for **grass**, **bath**, **basket**, etc.

Say words in singular (one item) and plural (more than one) – **hat**, **hats**; **peg**, **pegs**; **a dog**, **six dogs** – and encourage the pupil to *hear* that, by putting an **s** after a word, we make the word that means more than one of whatever it is.

Also show how the **s** is used in verbs: **run/runs**, **hit/hits**, **dig/digs**. **Tom zips his zip up.**

Explain that we say: **I run, you run** but **he runs; I dig, you dig** but **he digs**. Show where and why we use **s** in these ways. Point out, at the same time, that we always give **I** a capital letter and pronounce it using the long 'I' sound.

Sing the alphabet. Touch each letter as you sing it. We still have to learn **q** and **y**.

STEP 25

y

Teach the letter **y**. The *sounds* from the *letter* **y** are both a consonant and vowels. At the beginning of a word or syllable (as in **yes, yellow, beyond, crayon**) **y** is a consonant. There are very few words like this. As a vowel, it can make the same two sounds that **i** makes: the long sound in **fly, cry, satisfy**; and the short sound in **happy** and **system**.

Most schools teach the *consonant* **y** (**y** says 'yer'), but this does not work with the many words ending in **y**: **happy, funny, quickly**. You can change **happy** to **happiness**, and it makes life easier for learners if the last sound in **happy** is like a short **i**. It is safer at first, for spelling, to teach the *vowel* **y** as far as we can. When children learn only 'yer' for y, they end up sounding happy as happ-yer, etc., and do not get the meaning. For practical purposes, if you sound out yellow as i-ellow (short sound of i), the blended result is the way we usually say yellow, and this means that children only have to learn two sounds for y, the same two (long and short) that they learn for i. While hardly any words start with y (consonant), hundreds of words have the vowel y in the middle and end. It also exchanges with i in ai (ay) and oi (oy). (See Steps 56-60.)

If you are teaching a class, you may be able to find names ending in short y among your pupils: Harry (pronounced Harri, not Harr-ee), Henry, Polly, Billy, Sandy, Betty, Jenny, Patsy.

Remind the child of the vowels that were introduced in Step 19: ay, ee, I, oh, you. Tell him that the other letters give us sounds called consonants. This is useful knowledge if/when you wish to make him aware of the CVC (consonant-vowel-consonant) pattern as in cat or VCCV (vowel-consonant-consonant-vowel) as in rabbit.

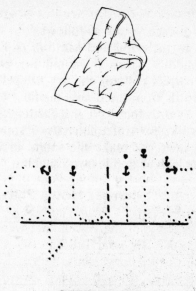

STEP 26

q

This is the *big day*, the very last letter, so do make a big fuss! In English words, the letter **q** is always followed by a **u**, and the two letters together say '**kw**'; or you can think of the **q** saying '**k**', and the **u** as its deep sound (as in **pull**). This works for getting the position of the lips right, etc.

Make the words: **quiz**, **quick**. Remind the pupil that the '**kw**' sound has the two letters **qu**.

Now the pupil is ready for the Bingo game. See page 183.

Spelling

It is a good idea if spelling can keep up with reading. I tell pupils they read with their ears, and, even more, they spell

with their ears (see page 12). Set out a grid with five
columns, one for each vowel, as follows.

Say a word to the pupil and ask him to listen for the
vowel in the middle. Which is the middle vowel? He can
then find the correct column and try to spell that word.
You can use words from the Bingo, the Dice Game, or the
Pairs pack; any words that have three letters/three sounds,
but not words like **fur** (three letters/two sounds) or **was**
where the **wa** does not make the sound in **wax**. Where
possible, let the learner do his own checking.

a	e	i	o	u
		zip		

The aim is plenty of practice so that the response to a
three-letter word becomes automatic and fast; not because
the pupil remembers the word-shape but because he is
blending the sounds.

Set out the loose individual alphabet letters on their own
letters on the large alphabet card. Get the pupil to pick out
the three letters needed for a word, arrange them correctly,
say the word and then put the letters back in their place.
Sing the alphabet.

It sounds silly to say that if someone learns quickly, he
will learn more quickly! But if too much time elapses (three

to four days) between one lesson and the next, the learning fades. But beyond that, if someone learns quickly, he is aware of his progress and that is an incentive. If the learning is slow, the pupil is not aware of progress and feels he is just plodding on without getting anywhere. An hour a day for ten days gives more progress than the same ten hours spread over 20 days.

Try out simple dictation, single words, phrases or sentences, like: **A dog can run. A pig is fat. Pat has a red hat. Jim got wet.** Make up your own.

Writing

If the child is pressing too hard when writing, turn the page over and let him feel the ridges he has made. Tell him that pressing hard will make him tired. Buy a cheap propelling pencil with a thin lead, so that it breaks when he presses too hard. This works when nagging does not.

Exercises

The following pages will give the pupil plenty of practice in reading and writing.

Draw a line from word to picture.

dot

lips

jug

mug

tap

gun

van

zip

fan

hat

six

6 :::

Unjumble the letters and write the word.

Six eggs
in a box

o
x
b   _ _ _

x
s
i   _ _ _

x
f
o   _ _ _

Is it a (b) or a (t)?

_b_ us

_b_ un

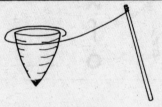

_t_ op

Is it a ⓑ or a ⓣ?

10

_t_ en

_b_ ox

_t_ ap

Jumbled words: Write the letters in the correct order.

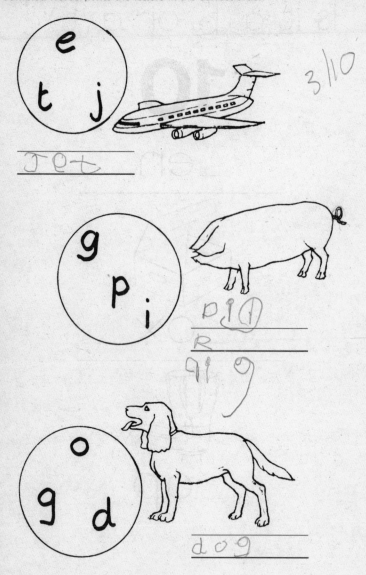

3/10

Jet

pig
R
gi g

dog

Jumbled words: Write the letters in the correct order. 3/10

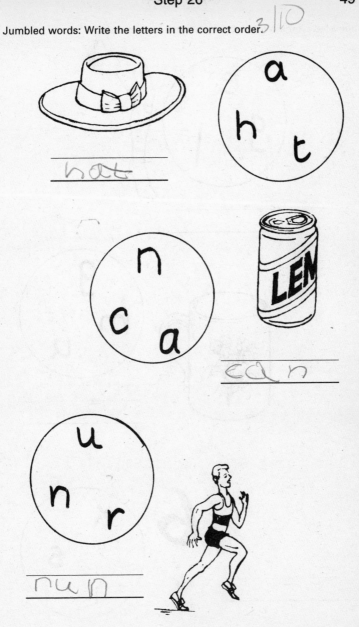

hat

a
h
t

can

n
c
a

LEM

run

u
n
r

Jumbled words: Write the letters in the correct order.

Say the word for the picture, and listen to the word as you say it. Then
spell it from listening to your own voice.

_____

_____

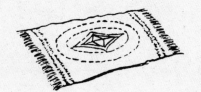

_____

_____

_____

_____

_____

_____

sun, sum, rug or mat, pan

Say the word for the picture, and listen to the word as you say it. Then spell it from listening to your own voice.

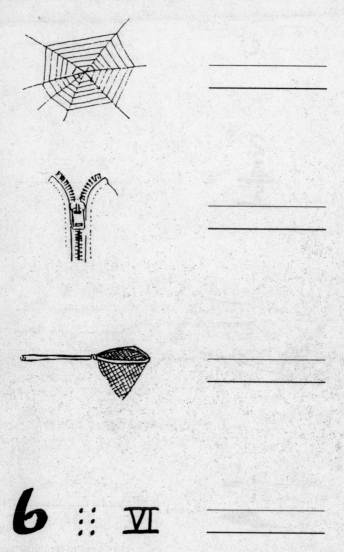

_____

_____

_____

_____

web, zip, net, six

Say the word for the picture, and listen to the word as you say it. Then spell it from listening to your own voice.

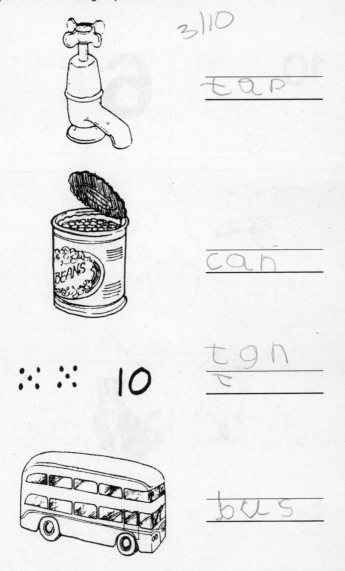

3/10

tap

can

tgn

bus

Can you put in the missing bits?

Show two words which are next to each other. Ask the pupil, 'Which letter has been changed in the second word, the first, middle or last? What is the new word?'

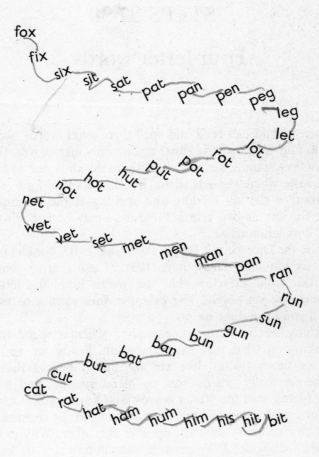

fox
fix
six sit sat pat pan pen peg
leg
let
lot
rot
pot
put
hut
hot
not
net
wet vet set met men man pan ran
run
sun
gun
bun
ban
bat
but
cut
cat
rat
hat ham hum him his hit bit

STEPS 27-30

Four-letter words

When a child can read and spell three-letter words, work with four-letter words, but, again, only use words that have four sounds, i.e. not **ship** where the **sh** is one sound, not **rake** where the **e** is silent. In schools spending 1½ to 3 hours a day on reading and spelling at the beginning just for one or two terms, three days may be enough for the four-letter stage.

Use the Dice Game, Bingo, Pairs and 'Is It?' booklet (see the section on Games, page 183). If using other workbooks, avoid exercises that use words involving letter-groups not yet taught. For example, **fork** cannot be used until you have done **or**.

Many teachers and some reading schemes spend time working on what they call 'consonant blends': **st**, **sp**, **tr**, **dr**, or 'letter-strings' like **str** and **spl**. I believe that if someone really grasps how to blend sounds, and read three-letter and four-letter words, and knows **s** and **t**, we do not need to spend extra time learning **st**. **St** consists of just two ordinary letters, one after the other. Why make it seem difficult? Why provide something extra to learn when we do not need it?

When we come, soon, to what I call letter-groups where two letters must be read together to make one sound, like **sh**, then is the time to have the pupil notice two letters together, but when reading **vest**, **flat**, **flag**, it is enough to go through the sequence of letters, sound them out and *listen*.

4/10/04

Words for Bingo
The words I use for four-letter Bingo are:

camp	fast*	flag
hand	rang**	sack
sand	rest	send
sent	vest	went
drip	fist	lick
limp	list	wink
pink	ring**	spin
wind	wing**	cost
drop	lock	song**
stop	lump	must
jump	just	

* Remind the pupil of the alternative pronunciation.
** **-ng** is a letter-consonant blend which sounds as *one* sound, a nasal. In **ring** you do not hear a hard **g** sound. **-ng** is sounded with the tongue down, back of mouth closed, and resonance in the nose. In certain two-syllable words (**an-gry**, **fin-ger**) the **g** begins a syllable and is hard.

The learner could listen to some of these words, choose the right column according to the vowel sound on the grid you made (see page 42) and write them in the appropriate column. He will also enjoy doing the following exercises.

You are given the first letter of the word. Can you write the word to match the picture?

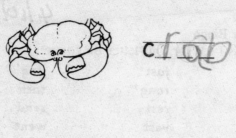

c _ _ _

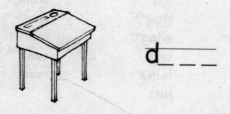

d _ _ _

f _ _ _

W _ _ _

crab, desk, frog, wing

You are given the first letter of the word. Can you write the word to match the picture?

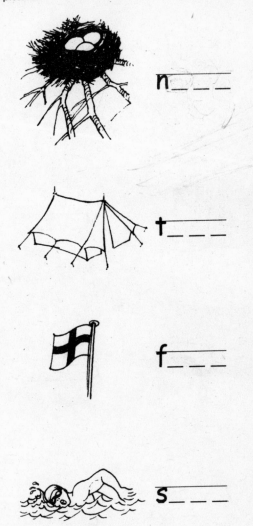

n _ _ _

t _ _ _

f _ _ _

s _ _ _

nest, tent, flag, swim

You are given the first letter of the word. Can you write the word to match the picture?

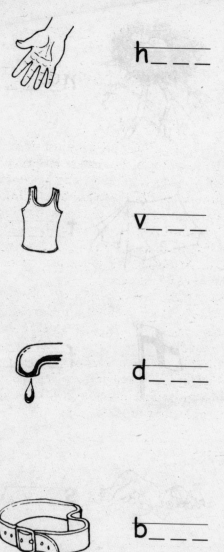

h _ _ _

v _ _ _

d _ _ _

b _ _ _

hand, vest, drip, belt

STEPS 31-35

Longer words

This is the last stage of reading with just single letters. You now move on to words of five letters: **stamp, crust, comic**, and then on to words of any length: **clinic, hospital, caravan, interesting, Japan, America, Canada**. Use your atlas. Many countries and towns have simply spelled names, and we must keep our pupil's mind and vocabulary expanding! Try **Scotland, Finland, India, Iran, Mexico, Italy, Brazil, Atlantic** and states in America: **Florida, Mississippi, Texas, Indiana**.

In some words we do not hear a clear vowel sound. We say **baskit, sev'n**. It is a good idea to say the word as it is spelt – **basket, seven** – making the **e** say the sound in **ten** for the first two or three times we say any word. Say: **hos-pi-tal (a** as in **cat); problem (e** as in **ten)**.

Some people need extra practice in listening to, and hearing, sounds in words (phonological awareness). Once a week, practise saying words as follows:

CRUST	c-rust
	cr-ust
	cru-st
	crus-t . . . **CRUST**.

The leader (teacher) begins the word, and the pupil completes it, saying the chunk needed to finish the word.

Then, later on, practise breaking words up into sounds:

church	ch ur ch
cloud	c l ou d
paint	p ai n t
play	p l ay

Play the Pairs Game, Dice Game and use the 'Is It?' booklet (see the Games section, page 183).

Words for Bingo
You can now make a further Bingo game, using the following words:

stamp	stand	swank
nasty*	flask*	grasp*
plank	seven	eleven
sting	bring	index
along	problem	trumpet
basket*	Frank	cramp
plant*	rabbit	rascal*
expand	empty	lemon
swing	drink	comic
bullet	hundred	rusty
crust	stump	

Remember: if you have a sound (letter) twice – for example, a **ck** – you only say the sound once. This also applies to double consonants, for example, **rabbit** (above) and many of the names opposite.

* Note regional variation.

Girls' names Bingo

Anna	Betty	Molly
Amanda	Brenda	Camilla
Olga	Pamela	Edna
Lydia	Stella	Vanessa
Rebecca	Kim	Sylvia
Linda	Peggy	Polly
Glenda	Matilda	Emma
Elsa	Veronica	Joanna
Hilda	Sally	Pat
Dolly	Hannah	Jessica
Mildred	Winifred	

Boys' names Bingo

Alan	Bill	Alec
Henry	Frank	Fred
Rex	Sam	Robin
Duncan	Kim	Kevin
William	Winston	Trevor
Brendan	Eric	Harry
Adam	Kit	Ronald
Tom	Colin	Derek
Tim	Jim	Max
Angus	Ross	Cliff
Jack	Patrick	

Get the child to try to spell the words and the names.

Reading and dictation
Try this:

Sam and his family on the sands.
Frank and Sam can swim. A red crab bit Sam. Frank
ran to Mum. Dad swam back to help Sam but the crab
still held on! Dad hit the crab and it let go. Sam put
the crab back on the sand. It ran fast.

Jokes
Jokes are usually short. They are funny (we hope). They
help learners grasp what a pun is. You can use them just
for reading, or for dictation. Many jokes are riddles,
starting with **What** or **Who**, so you will need to explain
that these are irregular words that do not match the
letter-sounds completely. (**What** comes under **wa**, Step
90.)
1.   What runs but has no legs? *A tap.*
2.   Can a hat box? *No, but a tin can.*
3.   What is a happy tin in the USA? *A-merry-can.*
4.   Miss: Did you spill the ink, Bill?
       Bill: Yes, I done it.
       Miss: Bill, where's your grammar?
       Bill: In bed with the flu.

(You will need to explain that the **e** in **done** is silent, does
not make the **o** long; and that **where** is an irregular word.)

5.   What has a bottom at the top? *A leg.*
6.   A book title: Willy Win, by Betty Wont. *(Will he win?*
       I bet he won't.)
7.   If a quadruped has 4 legs, and a biped has 2 legs, what
       is a zebra? *A stri-ped!*

Explain as necessary!

Bedtime stories

You can always read stories to children for their pleasure. Now you can start letting the learner read and puzzle out the words you know he can read – the words with no letter-groups. It gets really exciting when he says, 'No, let me do it by myself!' As he learns more letter-groups, he will read more of the words, until he can take over.

But if he starts guessing or predicting, discourage this, or stop story books for a while. The only 'don't' in my lessons is 'Don't guess'. Guessing is a real barrier to progress. It is a danger signal telling that the pupil cannot read from the letters. Pupils, sadly, think that guessing – fast – is better than getting it right at their own speed. But don't nag the child. Instead, I put out five sweets and each time the learner guesses, one sweet goes back in the jar. I do not say a word.

More practice

The crossword overleaf and the following exercises give the pupil plenty of practice of what he has been taught.

Crossword

Try a crossword. Read out the clues to the pupil. If he can't get one answer, go on to the next.

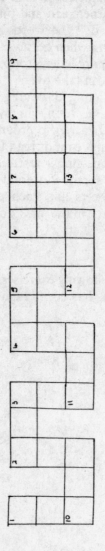

Clues across

2. I have . . a present.
4. The first colour of the rainbow.
6. We used to write with a . . . and ink.
8. Jerry is the mouse; Tom is the . . .
10. $2 \times 5 = \ldots$
11. A lady carries things in her hand- . . .
12. Water comes out of a . . . .
13. The end of your finger is your finger- . . .

Clues down

1. We hit a ball with a . . .
2. A soldier shoots with a . . .
3. Americans call a bath a . . .
4. A . . . is a small carpet.
5. We learn to write using . . . to . . . patterns.
6. A young dog is a . . .
7. We can have a Brazil . . ., hazel . . ., chest . . . .
8. The captain on a ship wears a . . . .
9. We climbed the hill to the very . . . .

Can you write the word beside the picture?

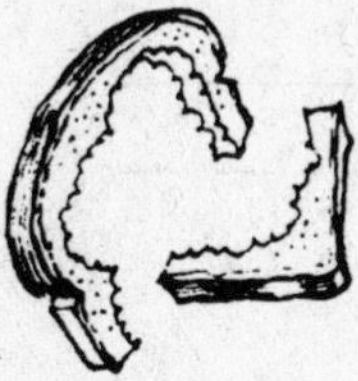

_____

_ _ _ _ _ _

_____

_ _ _ _ _ _

_____

_ _ _ _ _ _

_____

_ _ _ _ _ _

_____

_ _ _ _ _ _

plant, trumpet, stump, stamp, crust

C-A-T = CAT

Can you write the word beside the picture?

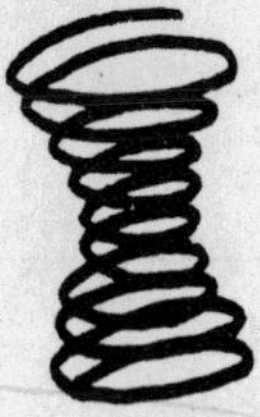

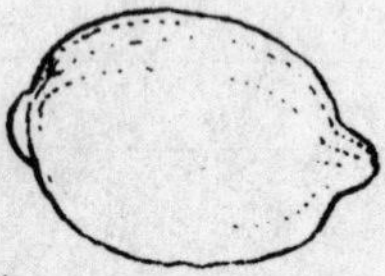

_____

_ _ _ _ _ _ _

_____

_ _ _ _ **O** _

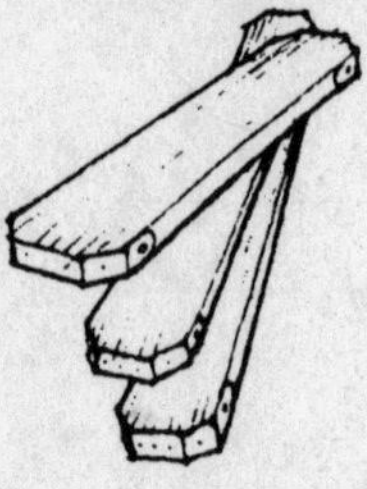

_____

_ _ _ _ _ _ _

_____

_ _ _ _ _ _ _

_____

_ _ _ _ _ _ _

spring, lemon, swing, basket, planks

Can you write the word beside the picture? If you have a sound (consonant) twice, you only say it once.

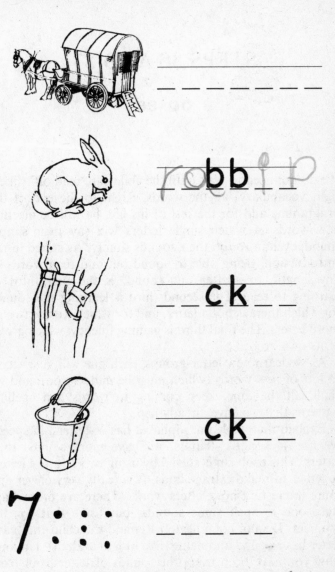

r o b b _ _

_ _ _ _ c k _ _

_ _ _ c k _ _

_ _ _ _ _ _

caravan, rabbit, bucket, seven

STEPS 36 AND 37

oo ee

We do not need to wait until the child can 'read off' (like a sight vocabulary) all the words. Right to the end of the programme and for the rest of his life, he will be meeting new words in which single letters will say their simple sound; even in **rough** the **r** sounds simply. As stated in the Introduction, being able to sound out and read words of any length, one letter one sound, is the first third of learning to read. The second third is learning the sounds for which there is not a letter, and for which we use two or more letters. The final third is gaining fluency, which grows of its own accord.

As we learn new letter-groups, each one will give access to lots of new words (which must be understood), and we shall, all the time, keep coming to words and spelling patterns that we have already had.

Explain that while our alphabet has 26 letters, in speech we use 44 sounds; that is, we have more sounds than letters. This problem is solved by using two or more letters together to make extra sounds. It is really very clever and quite interesting how letters work. (There are more ways than one to spell some sounds, but leave that for the moment. Do not complicate!) Remind the child that each letter has a sound and name (like **hhh** and **aitch**). Up until now you have been using the sounds of letters, but from now on when you are talking *about* letters, use their names:

hhh is the sound, **aitch** is the name.

The first two new sounds are **oo** and **ee**. Say: 'One **o** says **o** (as in **top**) but two **o's** say **oo** as in **moon**.' Have the child repeat three times, 'Two **o's** say **oo**'. Then ask, 'What do two **o's** say?' and 'If we want to write **oo**, what letters would we use?'

Find the pictures on page 78 with **oo** in them: **moon**, **hook**, **book**, **boot**, **room**. You can put each of these words and pictures onto one side of a small card, then list all the words on the other side, starting with the word shown in the picture on that card. Here and in later work, these 'sound cards' are the only material I use where the pupil can see the word and picture at the same time. I use them to give the pupil independence. If he forgets what **oo** says, he can go back to that card and work it out: **m..OO..n**, the sound after **m** is the sound **oo**. Have him read **moon**, **room**, **cool**, **stool**, then explain that sometimes the **oo**, although the same sound, is shorter, as in **book**, **hook**, **cook**, **good**, and have him read those words.

oo

mOOn
cool
soon
room
   look
   cook
   book
   good

ee

tree
feel
heel
week
seem
green
see
bee

The **ee** is simpler. 'Two **e's** say **eeee**.' When we sound out, we use *sounds*. When we are talking about letters, we use their names, so we say 'Two **eeee's** say **eeee**'. Have the pupil repeat this three times, then have him read the words in the list above. These are *not* to be learned but used as sounding out practice.

Sing the alphabet. Play the games made previously. Find the **ee** words on page 78.

Joined writing
You will see that on page 71 I have joined together the letters that must be said together. Your pupil may do the same, as an introduction to joined writing. Please yourself.

sh sh

fi **sh**

STEP 38

sh

Point out to the pupil that **h** is the blowy-letter. When you use it with another letter, you still blow – as in **sh**, **ch**, **th**. We first learn **sh**, the sound we make to tell people to **hush**. Have the pupil say **sh**, with his hand in front of his mouth, so that he can feel the wind of the blow. Have him say three times, '**Ess-aitch** says **sh**'. Have him complete the words listed below, and say each one, and understand it. Play games from previous lessons. Find the pictures on page 78 for **ship**, **fish**, **brush**, **shop**.

Write a joined **sh** on scrap paper, in large letters with a yellow felt pen or highlighter, and let the pupil go over the letters, to get the feel of how you join the letters. Draw the letters separately, then add the joining bit in a different colour, to show the extra line. If you wish, he can go over the words in the list in felt pen.

*fi***sh**

*fi*__   **cra**__   __**ip**   __**ut**

di__   **bru**__   __**op**   __**rimp**

*fla*__

chin _ch_ 🗣

14/11/04

STEP 39

ch

Read the words from the **sh** list. Remind him that **h** is a blowy letter. With **c**, it says a sound like a sneeze. **SH** goes on longer. **CH** stops short.

Have the pupil repeat three times, '**See-aitch** says **ch**'. Show that the picture is of a chin, and have the pupil find the **ch** in that word.

Have the pupil complete the words below, read and understand them.

_ch_ in	mu_ch_	fet_ch_
_ch_ ips	su_ch_	dit_ch_
_ch_ op	ri_ch_	mat_ch_
_ch_ ap	crun_ch_	scrat_ch_

Point out that **such**, **much**, **rich**, just end in **ch**, but other words with a short vowel are spelt -**tch**: **patch**, **fetch**, **hitch**, **Scotch**, **hutch**. See also Step 66, page 137.

Sing the alphabet. Play the previous games.

Write a large **ch** in a pale colour, joined, and have the learner go over it, to learn how to join. Find the pictures for **ch** on page 78 (**chips**, **match**).

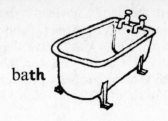

bath

STEP 40

th

Good speech helps good spelling. Tell the pupil that **th** is another letter-group with an **h** in it, so there will be a blow in the way you sound it. In **th** the **t** stands for **tongue**, so have the child put the tip of his tongue out and then blow, to make the sound of **th**.

Go back over a few pairs of letters: **t/d, p/b, k/g**. Have the pupil put his hand on his throat, to feel that with the first letter of each of these pairs there is no tremble, but when we say **d, b, g** (in **go**), our throat vibrates (and they learn what **vibrate** means) because they are *voiced*. (The **t** must be just **t** and not **ter**, for this to work. **Ter** is two sounds, **t** and **er**, and the **er** is voiced.)

Today's letter-group can be both voiced (with tremble) and unvoiced. Have the pupil say the first words with unvoiced **th**, then voiced, in **this, then, that**. For **the**, say, '**Tee-aitch-ee** says **the**'.

The pupil will sound out **bath**, but, when he realises its meaning, may change it to '**bah . . .th**' or '**barth**' if he lives in the south of the UK, or to '**baff**' (heard all over the UK now). So we must explain that there is no such word as **baff**, that for **th** we must put out the tip of the tongue (think '**t** for **tongue**, **h** for **blow**'), but for ***f*** we bite the bottom lip. Have the pupil say clearly: **deaf** (cannot hear) and **death** (no longer alive); **three** (3) and **free** (we did not have to pay for it). For a class, have the whole class say these words very distinctly, and for the next fortnight check that the **th** is being properly pronounced.

Get the pupil to fill in the gaps below:

bath

ba____	____ink	____en
pa____	____is	____em
wi____	____at	____e

Have the pupil find the pictures for the words **teeth** and **bath** on page 78. He has now found all the pictures on that page and can now say the word for each picture, choose the correct column and write the word. Check that the pupil is saying **teeth**, not **teef**, and so on.

We have now had **oo**, **ee**, **sh**, **ch**, **th**, and it is time to use (make) more games – Pairs, Bingo, the Dice Game, and 'Is It?' book – using all five letter-groups. (See the Games section, page 183.)

Words for Bingo

been	chips	chop
chunk	cheek	feed
fetch	fish	food
good	green	hood
look	much	pool
sheep	shop	sweet
shot	shut	ship
seem	spoon	teeth
tooth	sheets	tree
think	this	thick
that	week	

You can also dictate them one at a time, and have the child choose the column they should go in (**teeth** could go under **ee** or **th**). Remind the writer not to press too hard. Check the pencil-grip.

Jokes
1. What is the biggest moth? *A mam-moth.*
2. What do you get when you plant a gun? *Lots of shoots.*
3. What is long, has a pink hat, and lies in a box? *A match.*

Exercise
Get the pupil to say the word for each picture overleaf, listen to the word, and then write it in the column with the matching sound on page 79.

tree, book, room, heel, bee, brush, chips, shop, boot, fish, bath, ship, match, teeth (can go in two columns), street, moon, hook.

th	ch	sh	ee	oo

STEP 41

ar

The next five letter-groups are vowel + **r**. The vowels are very important. The pupil can now learn the names of the vowels, which are the long sounds:

a (ay)   **e (ee)**   **i (I)**   **o (oh)**   **u (you)**

When you sing the alphabet, you are singing the names of the letters. When we sound out, we use letter-sounds, but when we talk about letters, you should now be using their names, occasionally reminding the pupil that, '**aitch** says **hhh**' and so on.

Ar (**ay-ar**) says the sound in **car** and **or** as in **fork**. Children seem to find these easier to learn than the **er**, **ir**, **ur**, which all make the same sound (**term**, **bird**, **curl**). If you wish to go slowly, do the **ar**, **or**, first and then the other three. If your pupil seems to be mopping it all up very easily, you can try the five together. Use your judgment.

Ar: The mouth is fairly wide open for this. Try to make the **r** audible. Scottish reading attainment regularly comes out better than English and I wonder if this is due to their clearer sound of the **r**. Try to say **carr** rather than **cah**. Most Americans sound the **r**. Look in the mirror, and see if your lips move forward towards the end of the sound, as they should. Exaggerate the **r** at the end of all five groups, for the next fortnight. Including words like **sharp** emphasises to the pupil that letter-groups (like **sh**) once learned keep coming in.

**ar
arm**

Get the pupil to fill in the gaps in the following:

ar

_____m   sh_____p

p_____k   f_____m-y_____d

st_____t   p_____t

Joke
What did the jack say to the car? '*Can I give you a lift?*'
(**Give**: explain that English words do not end in **v** so you have to put an **e** after.)

STEP 42

or

Have the pupil write in **or** in the examples below and read out loud each word.

or
fork

or

f____k	m____ning
st____m	n____th
sh____t	c____k
c____n	

For **or** the mouth is not so wide-open as for **ar**. Again, try to sound the **r** so that **pour/pore** does not sound like **paw**. If it is **pouring with rain** the word **pouring** does not sound the same as if a cat is **pawing a mouse** (with no **r** sound). Try also **soaring/sawing**. Play the previous games. Use 'Is It?', the Dice Game, Bingo and Pairs for **ar**, **or** words.

ar, or
Get the pupil to complete the following words by writing in
ar:

b____n   ____ch

c____   c____ds

d____t   st____

c____pet

Then get him to complete these words by writing in **or**:

f____k   h____se

p____ch   t____ch

st____k

Now get him to write each word next to the correct picture
on the following pages.

Words for Bingo

charm	spark	smart
party	hardly	carpet
barn	target	sharp
farm-yard	alarm	market
darling	north	corner
sport	lord	stork
horse	storm	morning
born	forget	cork
form	short	before
Gordon	Norma	porch
escort	Ford	

———————————

———————————

———————————

———————————

———————————

———————————

———————————

———————————

_____
_____

_____
_____

_____
_____

_____
_____

_____
_____

_____
_____

_____
_____

_____ _e_
_____

STEPS 43, 44 AND 45

er ir ur

These three-letter groups all sound the same. Look in the mirror to check that your lips come forward, sides of mouth *in*.

er: As well as words in the Bingo list, you can show how we make a comparative using **-er**, and a superlative ending in **-est**:

Positive	Comparative (+ **er**)	Superlative (+ **est**)
fast	faster	fastest
quick	quicker	quickest
long	longer	longest
strong	stronger	strongest
rich	richer	richest

Choose your words with care. Avoid **wet** because the **t** has to be doubled in **wetter**, **wettest**, and we have not yet taught doubling. Avoid **wide**, **late**, etc, because we have not yet taught what the **e** does. Just say, for now, that in many words that end in **-er**, the consonant in front is doubled: **hammer**, **spanner**, **better**, **letter**, **pepper**, **slipper**, **grasshopper**, **butter**.

-er is by far the most common spelling for this sound, then **-ir**, with **-ur** least common. They are all easy to read, but we have to remember which we need for spelling. If you teach reading from sounds to letters, there will be about five choices for the long **a** sound with many dilemmas over which one to use. If you teach reading as this book does, from letters to sounds, there are dilemmas in the **er** sound, **ea**, **ou**, **ow**, **ough**, and homophones (words like **steel/steal**; **there/their**), but you are on much surer ground than using a scheme that works back from sounds to letters.

Get the pupil to fill in the gaps.

hammer	bird	church
f__n	sk__t	f__
t__m	sh__t	b__n
hamm__	g__l	t__n
butt__	b__d	c__l
fast__	th__ty	h__t
ladd__	f__m	m__m__
spann__	th__st	sp__t

Words for Bingo

born	faster	morning	thirty
bird	forty	person	turn
charm	fur	sparkling	corner

barn	murmur	card	jerk
corn	shirt	burst	nurse
father	sport	curl	skirt
firm	thirsty	fork	term
important	dart	farm	thorn

Explain that **father** is irregular in the way we say the **a**.

Jokes

1. Why did the lobster blush? *Because he saw the salad dressing.* (Explain **au** and **aw**, Steps 74 and 75.)
2. 'Peter, I hope I didn't see you copying just then!'
   'I hope you didn't as well!'
3. Miss: Mark, where does your mum come from?
   Mark: Alaska.
   Miss: Don't bother. I'll ask her myself.

Practice

Get the pupil to practise saying the following words, then write them beside the correct picture on the following pages.

er:

fern	river	hammer
ladder	finger	swimmer
jumper	spanner	

ir:

| shirt | blackbird | skirt |
| thirty | | |

ur:

church	nurse	burglar
turnip	purse	spurs
turkey	fur	

_____
_____

_____
_____

_____
_____

_____
_____

_____
_____

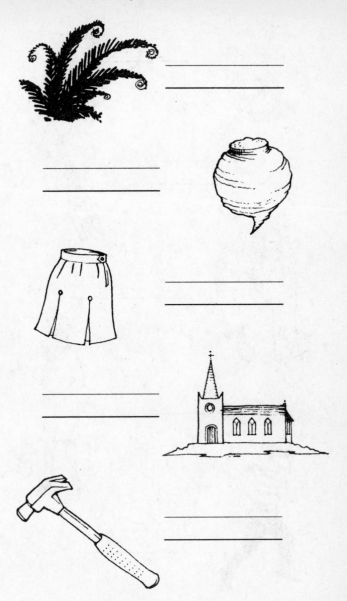

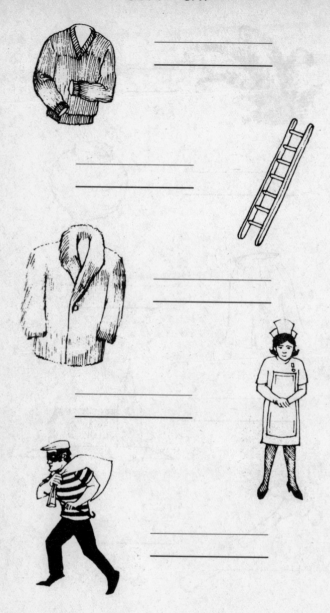

_____

_____

_____

_____

_____

_____

_____

_____

_____

_____

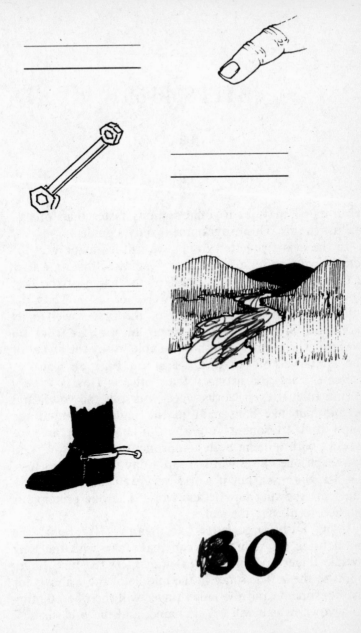

STEPS 46-50

-e

Your pupil may learn some sections faster than others. Adjust to this. This programme is only a guide.

In the next five-letter groups we will learn the way the letter **e** works after a vowel. Step 37 showed that an **e** after **e** (two **e's**) says **ee**, the sound of the name of the first vowel. This works for all the vowels, not just **e**. Thus, the following **e** changes the sound of the first vowel to its name: **ae** (Scottish **Mae**), **ee** (tree), **ie** (pie), **oe** (toe), **ue** (value). The pupil should now be able to say the *names* of the five vowels off pat: **a, e, i, o, u** (**ay, ee, I, oh, you**).

Some rules are stronger than others. This is a very strong rule. It even works when you split the vowel and **e**, and put one consonant in the middle. Remind the pupil that consonants are the 20 letters that are not vowels, with **y** being both a consonant and a vowel. You can teach one vowel word-group a day for five days (**a-e, e-e, i-e, o-e, u-e**), but it works very well to teach all five together, showing how letters work. The one principle is applied to all five the same.

Using fairly large letters, as in an 'Is It?' book, the pupil using his right hand can make a **v** with the long middle finger and first (index) finger: let the long finger point to the **e**. The space in the middle of the **v** allows for the consonant, and the index finger will then be pointing to a vowel which will say its name, and the **e** is silent. **E** is silent at the end of English words. (Café is French and the **e** has an accent. Two **e's** we do sound: **coffee**, **settee**.) Try it on **cake**. The long finger points to the **e**, the **k** is in the space and the index finger points to the **a** which says its name, and you sound out:

c...a.....e (the **e** is silent)
k.

The last sound is **k**, the last letter is **e**.

Play the Pairs game, Bingo and the Dice Game; use the 'Is It?' booklet.

Words for Bingo
These can include pairs like **cod/code**, **pin/pine**, **fad/fade**, **hop/hope**, even **fir/fire**, to make the reader notice if there is a final **e** or not, or they can all be **-e** words:

cane	these	pine
toe	blue	shame
even	time	open
clue	paper	Peter
fine	over	rescue
skate	concrete	wine
rope	tube	plate
extreme	tiger	stone
fumes	game	theme
wire	those	pure
gate	excuse	

Practice
Get the pupil to write in the vowels on pages 96-98.

C-A-T = CAT

Mae
Praed

a.e

gate

see
tree

e.e

10   4
2   8   6

even
numbers

c__k__   __v__ning
g__m__   th__s__
m__k__   th__m__
sp__d__   St__v__
sk__t__s   concr__t__
pl__t__   Cr__t__
p__p__r   extr__m__
s__m__
f__d__
c__p__

pie	toe
tie	hoe
i.e	o.e

pipe	rose
w__p__	n__s__
r__p__	h__s__
str__p__s	th__s__
w__n__	r__p__
t__m__	h__p__
t__g__r	st__n__
l__k__	h__m__

value
tissue

u.e

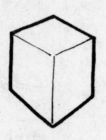

cube

t__b__
f__m__s
__s__
am__s__
exc__s__
fl__t__
comp__t__r
ref__s__
incl__d__

Get the pupil to add the vowels below, then to write the correct word beside each picture on pages 100-102.

Note **here** (regular) but **there** (irregular).

a.e

g_t_s   sp_d_   wh_l_   sn_k_

i.e

k_t_   sp_r_   d_v_   sl_d_   w_n_

o.e

n_s_   gl_b_   c_n_   b_n_   tadp_l_

u.e

t_b_   fl_t_

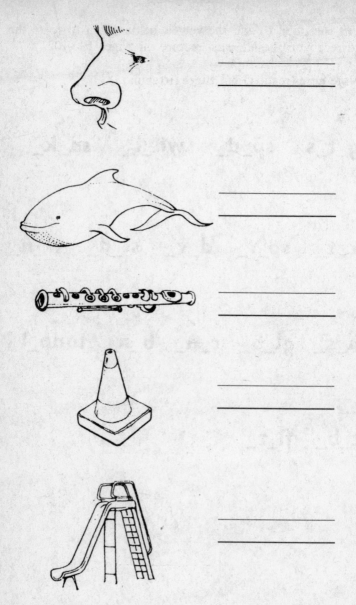

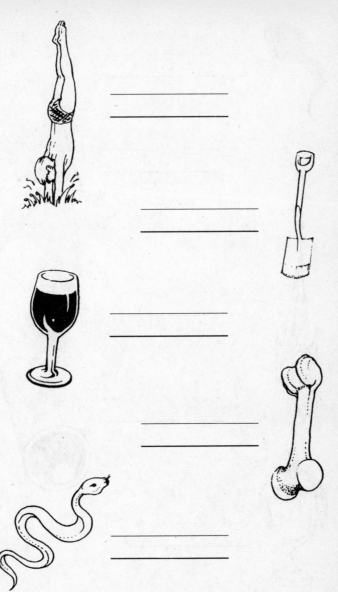

_____
_____

_____
_____

_____
_____

_____
_____

_____
_____

So that earlier learning does not fade, it is time now to begin each lesson revising earlier work. Starting from Step 27, each day get the pupil to practise reading, writing and spelling the words introduced in one Step. Put in the date to show which ones you have done.

STEP 51

Doubling

Read through this section. You may decide to leave it until later for very young children aged three or four, but, for older children and adults, this section is very useful at this point as a way of making them consider letters/sounds and to stop them guessing for meaning. This emphasises that reading is all about letters – a particular sequence of letters.

E can 'jump back over one letter' and make a previous vowel say its name, but cannot jump over two letters. Consider: **rip/ripper/ripe**, **bet/better/Peter**, **cut/cutter/cute**, **whip/whippet/wipe**. When you want the short **a** to remain short, when you want to keep the sound of **pat** in **patter**, you cannot just put **er** after **pat**, because you would then have **a-e**, **pater**. Because the **e** cannot jump back over two letters, you double the consonant in between, which then makes a wall, and the later **e** cannot jump back over it. Play around with these words:

rip, **ripe**   **trip**, **tripe**
ripping   **tripping**

strip   **stripe**   **stripped**, **striped**
stripping   **striping**

Consider comparatives ending in **-er**, and superlatives ending in **-est**:

	wide	wider	widest
	safe	safer	safest
	fine	finer	finest
but	fat	fatter	fattest
	thin	thinner	thinnest
Try	hot	h_____	h_____
	big	b_____	b_____

When you want a double **k**, you put **-ck**:

baker	packing	packet	cracker	jacket
	pecking	Becket		
biker	licking	wicket	cricket	ticket
joker	locking	pocket	locket	socket
duke	sucking	bucket		

It is not just the vowel **e** that can affect a previous vowel. *Any* vowel can make a vowel two letters earlier say its name, and **y** is a vowel. Consider:

pupil/puppet	duty/putty	duly/dully
acorn/accord	holy/holly	uniform/bunny

This is useful, but it is not a 100% rule; there are exceptions. Sometimes we can have VCV (vowel-consonant-vowel) and the first vowel is short: **atom**, **lemon**, **robin**, but looking at it the other way, when we *do* have a double consonant, the vowel in front is always short: **button**, **patter**, **borrow**, **yellow**, **marry** (cf **Mary**). Because **i** works like **e**, when you add **-ing** you drop the **e**. You do not need both.

Root word	-ing	-ed	-er
hop	hopping	hopped	hopper (-pp)
hope	hoping	hoped	hoper

Get the pupil to try to finish the following words:

strip	str____	str____	str____
stripe	str____	str____	str____
mat	m____	m____	m____
rub	r____	r____	r____
trim	t____	t____	t____

Now get him to try these. Should he double the last consonant, drop the **e**, or does he make no change at all before he adds the ending (suffix)?

wipe	w____	w____	w____
lick	l____	l____	l____
stop	s____	s____	s____
rust	r____	r____	
bake	b____	b____	b____
fetch	f____	f____	f____
wish	w____	w____	w____

Notice:
like, liked, liking
rake, raked, raking

but
lick, licked, licking
rack, racked, racking

Jokes and riddles

1. How can you communicate with a fish? *Drop him a line.*
2. Two boys were born on the same day, on the same date, to the same set of parents. They look alike, think alike, and behave alike, yet they are not twins. What are they? *They are 2 of a set of triplets.*
3. What kind of snake is good at sums? *An adder.*

STEPS 52, 53 AND 54

-le

The next letter-group, **-le**, follows on very easily after **-e** and doubling. **-le** is the only other letter-arrangement that does the same thing as **e** (or any vowel), that is, it can 'jump back' over one letter, but not two, to make a vowel say its name.

Look at the following two columns. There are the five vowels in each column, and all the words end in **-le**, but the **a**, **e**, **i**, **o** and **u** in the first column have the long vowel sound, and in the second the short sound. There are not many of the first kind; most **-le** words have the short vowel sound. **Needle**, **feeble**, have two **e's** and would say a long **ee** anyway. The only example I can find to fit this pattern for the long **e** with only one **e** is Keble, which is the name of a college of Oxford University.

table	**raffle**
Keble	**pebble**
trifle	**little**
noble	**bottle**
bugle	**struggle, snuggle**

When the letters between the vowel and the **-le** are **-st-**, the vowel is short and the **t** is silent:

castle	**pestle** (& mortar)	**whistle**	**jostle**	**rustle**

(Of course, some people pronounce **castle** as **cahstle** making an **ah** sound.)

When there is a **c** between the vowel and **-le**, except in the name of the town **Acle**, the vowel is short:

miracle   obstacle   oracle   spectacles   particle

When using the 'Is It?' booklet, or reading any **-le** words in large print, use the same routine of making fingers into a **V**, the long finger point to the **-le**, a space for the (one or two) consonant(s), and the index finger will then point to a vowel. Is the vowel long (one consonant in the space) or short (two consonants in the space)?

   Teaching how the letters work helps to keep attention on the letters, the sequence, the direction and the sounds (and off illustrations, which can distract). This stage should be short and easy. Do not wait until the pupil can spell every word. Go on when he can read the words and play Bingo comfortably. Play the other games too.

Words for Bingo

apple	pebble	thimble	bottle	uncle
battle	settle	little		jungle
crackle	tremble	twinkle		purple
castle		whistle		cuddle
handle		simple		puzzle
		middle		struggle

Words ending in -ible and **-able** break the rule: the **i/a** is short: **possible, terrible, visible, drinkable, tolerable.**

table		title	noble	bugle
		Bible		
		rifle		

Jokes

1. Why is a pig like (a bottle of) ink? *Because it goes in a pen.*
2. 'What is another name for a pig's skin?'
   'Dunno, miss.'
   'Hide, girl, hide!'
   'Quick, kids, under the table!'

Tongue-twister

Peter Piper picked a peck of pickled peppers. Where's the peck of pickled peppers Peter Piper picked?

Exercise

Get the pupil to complete the following words and match each one to the appropriate picture on the following pages.

app__   padd__   thimb__

bott__   hand__   dimp__

bang__   fidd__   kett__

cand__   rectang__   scribb__

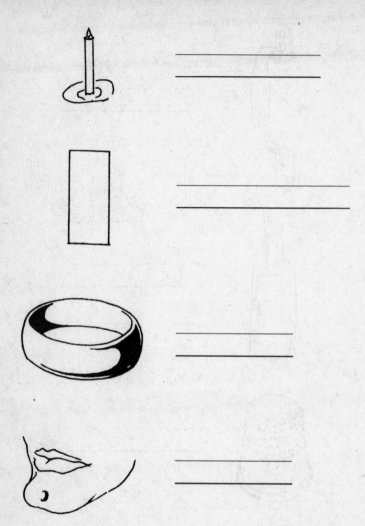

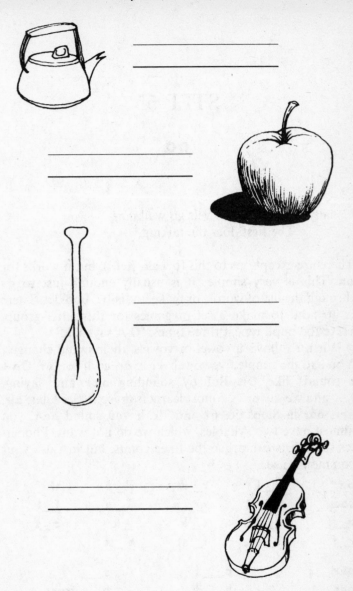

STEP 55

oa

Usually, 'When two vowels go walking,
            The first does the talking.'

There are exceptions to this (**break**, **field**), but it works for
oa. This is very simple. It is usually enough just to go
through the list of words, or make an 'Is It?' booklet. There
is no need to make a set of games for this letter-group.
Have the pupil repeat three times, '**O-A** says **Oh**!'
    When **r** follows a vowel or vowels, their sound changes.
You had the simple five vowels +r in **ar**, **er**, **ir**, **or**, **ur**. **Oa** +
r sounds like **Or**. But by sounding **oh-r** and saying,
'. . . and we say **or** . . .' most learners grasp it. See later, **air**,
ear, **our** in Steps 56, 61 and 70. If you sound **oa-r**, you
almost have two syllables, which we do not want. Phonetics specialists can argue the finer points, but just use your
common sense.

oa:	c__l	r__d	fl__t	thr__t
soap	m__n	gr__n	J__n	f__l
b__t	g__l	s__k	__k	c__t
l__f	c__st	r__st	t__st	

oar:	b___d		s___
oar	h___d		h___ frost
boar			

STEPS 56-60

i, y; ai, ay; oi, oy

Revision
Remember, every day, to get the pupil to read through one set of words learnt earlier in the programme and keep a note of the date so that you know when you revised them.

Practice with long words
Sound out a longish word (as you did for **crust** on page 61) and see if the pupil can complete it:

splendid	**s . . . plendid**
	sp . . . lendid
	spl . . . endid
	sple . . . ndid
	splen . . . did
	splend . . . id
	splendi . . . d
	splendid!

Words ending in i
Learning one spelling *rule* 'unlocks' dozens of words. There is a rule: No English word ends in **q, u, v, j** or **i**. This section is about the last one. **Ski** is a Norwegian word, **spaghetti**, **macaroni** and **broccoli** are Italian. **Taxi** is half

of **taxicab**. In the word **I**, **I** is the beginning, middle and end.

Words ending in y

If a word ends with **y**, look carefully at what happens when we add extra letters and sounds to it at the end. You change the **y** into **i** when you add on at the end:

Adjective

| **happy** | **happily** | **happier** | **happiest** | **happiness** |

Verbs

| **hurry** | **hurries** | **hurried** | *but* | **hurrying*** |
| **worry** | **worries** | **worried** | *but* | **worrying*** |

*as we cannot have two **i**'s together, except in a non-English word like **ski-ing**.

The long **i** sound:

| **cry** | **cries** | **cried** | **crying** |
| **reply** | **replies** | **replied** | **replying** |

Nouns

| **pony** | **ponies** | **cherry** | **cherries** |
| **fly** | **flies** | | |

This works whether the word is adjective, noun or verb, and whether the **y** is long or short.

    You cannot have **i** at the end, but you can have **y** anywhere. At the beginning of a word or syllable, **y** is a consonant (**yes**, **beyond**). Elsewhere it is a vowel, making the same sounds as **i**.

Y *saying the short sound*

funny	sill_	m_th
s_rup	m_ster_	s_stem
p_jamas	p_ramid	d_slexia
famil_		

Y *saying the long sound*

h_drant	d_namo	satisf_
repl_	p_thon	d_namite
def_	den_	verif_
multipl_		

i/y in ai/ay, oi/oy

I and **y** can be part of a letter-group, and they keep the same rules: you can't have **i** at the end. **AI** says the long **a** sound as in **sail**, but, at the end of a word, it has to be **ay**, as in **tray**. **OI** says the sound in **coin**, but at the end it is **oy** as in **boy**. Have the pupil say three times:

'You can't have **i** at the end', then

'**a-i** says **ay**, **a-y** (**ay-wye**) at the end', then

'**o-i** says **oi**, **o-y** (**oh-wye**) at the end.'

Work through an exercise, then play a game. As the pupil reads through the lists of words, he must say each word, pronounce it correctly, and either know what it means, tell you if you are not sure he understands it, or he must *ask*. Many children think that saying the word is enough, and do not ask for the meaning. Asking must be strongly encouraged. Make sure they realise that asking for the meaning is a sign of intelligence and common sense, not a sign of being stupid. Indeed, it *is* stupid to jump over words, saying them without understanding.

r-controlled ai

As with other vowel groupings, when **r** follows **ai**, the sound changes slightly. **Air**, **chair**, **fair**, should be one syllable and not **ay-er**. Once the pupil gets used to **air**, it will be easily read in other words. (**Oir** is rare: **choir** is pronounced **kwire**, **quire**, and is an irregular word.) There should be a sound in **air** rather like **ai**: if **fair hair** is pronounced as **fur her**, encourage more of an **ai** (long **a**) sound in the **air**. In **said**, the spelling is regular; it is the pronunciation that is irregular.

Sing the alphabet. Read through a column of words introduced earlier. Play the games. Get the child to read the 'Is It?' words, then see if he can spell them and words from earlier work.

Words for Bingo

aim	maintain	holiday	noise	boy
chair	obtain	play	spoil	enjoy
nail	pain	Thursday	point	annoy
railway	rain	Sunday	join	royal
entertain	train	stray	foil	
explain	strain	pray	coin	
		tray	boil	
		ray	coil	

Jokes (for dictation)
1. What does a cat do when it rains? *It gets wet.*
2. Who drives all his customers away? *A taxi-driver.*

Practice
Get the pupil to try the following.

Get the pupil to practise saying these words:

ai	ay
s ai l	tr ay
ai m	pl ay
n ai ls	pr ay
h ai r	Sun d ay
up st air s	holi d ay
ex pl ai n	spr ay
ex cl ai m	cr ay on

Get the pupil to practise saying these words:

oi   oy

c oi n   t oy

b oi l   b oy

sp oi l   en j oy

j oi n t   a nn oy

t oi l et   des tr oy

p oi n t   oy st er

ai, ay; oi, oy

_____

_____

_____ **ing**

_____

_____

_____

_____

_____

_____

ai, ay; oi, oy

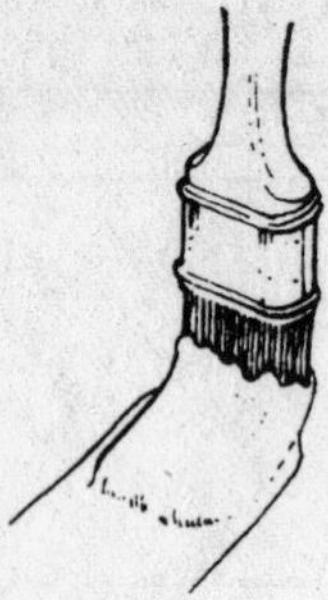

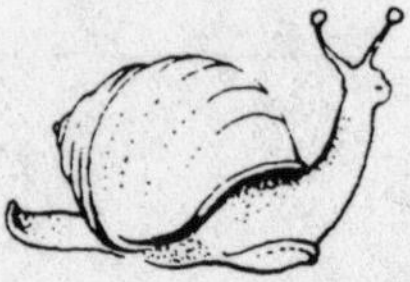

_____

_____

_____

_____

_____

_____

_____

_____

_____

_____

_____

_____

paint-brush, saint, chain, trailer, snail

ai, ay; oi, oy

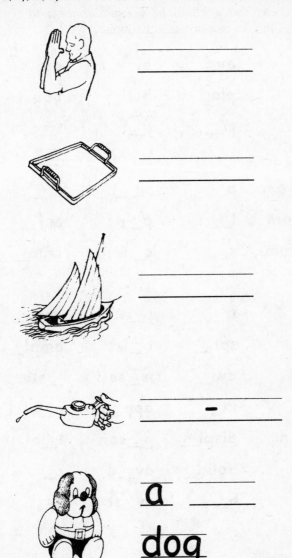

a
dog

pray, tray, sail, oil-can, a toy dog

Get the pupil to write the letter-group in the space, for each column and say the word. If he doesn't understand the meaning, get him to ask or use a dictionary.

ai	ay	oi	oy
paint	play	boil	boy
tr__n	cl__	f__l	t__
p__d from	p__	sp__l	R__
l__d from	l__	p__nt	enj__
s__d from	s__	c__n	ann__
ag__n	tr__	j__nt	destr__
afr__d	spr__	t__let	empl__
expl__n	aw__	n__se	__ster
obt__n	m__	app__nt	r__al
m__nt__n	displ__	p__son	l__al
f__l	holid__	av__d	c__
n__l	h__	m__st	

i, y; ai,ay; oi, oy

Copy the grid below. Get the pupil to read the following words, then write each one in the correct column. Get him to write the word without looking (copying) if he can and to ask the meaning of any new words.

boy, chain, toy, trailer, boiling, spray, waiter, paid, snail, coil (of rope), tail, joint (in wood), coin, pointing, oil-can, hay, pray, tray, royalty, oyster, fray, play, destroy

ai	ay	oi	oy

STEPS 61 AND 62

ea

Letter-groups which are consistent and reliable are easier to learn. We can say 's-h says sh' and it will, every time (except in the words **mis-hap** and **mis-hit**, not much used by beginning readers). However, **ea** is not consistent. There are many words where **ea** says the same sound as **ee**, and many others where it says the short sound as in **head**. Make (or use) an 'Is It?' book with both sounds, and tell the pupil to try the **ee** sound first; if that does not produce a real word, try the short **e**. **Peas** – the long **ee** works; **leather**, try **leether** which is not a word, so try **lether** and that is the sound. There is no rule as to which is which. In a few words, the same letters give different-sounding words: **Can you read it? I have read it. A lead pencil. Lead the way.**

ea (ee)	ea (e)
sea	bread
b____ch	h____ven
p____ch	h____d
str____m	st____dy
app____r	w____ther

You have already learned that the five vowels change their sound when followed by an **r**. We say they are **r**-controlled. **Ea** can also be **r**-controlled producing three different sounds:

In four words, **ear** sounds like **air**:
   bear, pear, wear, tear.
In a few words, **ear** sounds like **er**:
   earn, learn, early, earth, search, pearl, heard, yearn.
In two words, **ear** sounds like **ar**:
   heart, hearth.
In other words, **ear** sounds the same as **eer**:
   ear, year, fear, dear, appear.

Words for Bingo

please	reason	steal
easy	clean	meat
leave	feast	least
fear	breathe	near
year	teach	appear
dear		

deaf	bread	dreadful
ready	jealous	thread
steady	weather	feather
instead	healthy	spread
tread	weapon	heavy
sweat		

Jokes (for dictation)
1. Teacher: Why are you late, Kevin?
    Kevin: I was dreaming about this football match, and it went into extra time so I had to stay asleep to see the finish.

2.   'Frank,' said the weary maths master, 'If you had £7 in one pocket and £7 in another, what would you have?'

    'Someone else's jeans on!' Frank replied.

3.   Cookery Teacher: Jane, how can we stop food from going bad?

    Jane: By eating it, miss.

4.   'Did you hear about the fool who keeps saying "No"?'

    'No'.

    'Oh, so it's you.'

5.   What's the difference between a railway train and a tree? *One leaves its shed, and the other sheds its leaves.*

More practice

Get the pupil to complete the following words by writing in **ea**, then write the word beside the appropriate picture on the following pages:

j____ns   **p____k**   **sp____r**

m____t   **str____m**   **sw____ter**

____gle   **br____d**   **b____ds**

thr____d   **sh____rs**   **b____rd**

s____   **s____t**   **t____-pot**

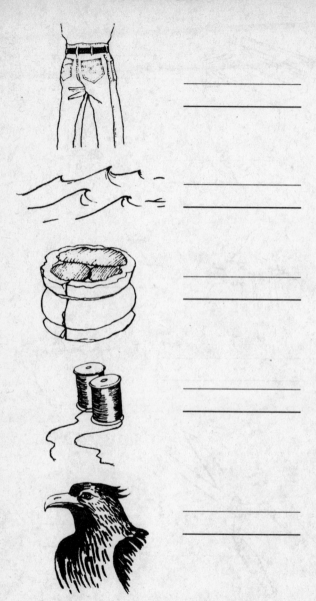

STEPS 63-68

Soft **c**, **g**

I have allocated six steps for this but it may take longer for the child to learn.

The pupil has by now had a lot of practice in making a **c** say '**kuh**', and a **g** say its hard sound as in **go**; but he has also met **ch** as in **chop**. **C** and **g** are the only two letters of the alphabet that can be *hard* and *soft*. The sound we learned first, as in **cat**, **dog**, is the *hard* sound. The *soft* sound is the sound in their name, **cee** and **jee**, so that **c** sounds like '**sss**' and **g** sounds like '**j**'. They say this soft sound when followed by **e**, **i** or **y**. This gives us six letter-groups: **ce**, **ci**, **cy**; **ge**, **gi**, **gy**. You can either take them one at a time, or explain the general principle and let the pupil try out all six, and go on from there.

When soft **c** and **g** are introduced, some learners try to change every **c/g** into the new, soft sound. Tell them that all the words where **c** and **g** have previously said the hard sound will go on saying it, that we are not changing any words we have had already, but looking at new words.

Write the two letters in joined writing if you wish. This helps to imprint on the learner's mind that they go together. You will see that in the columns on pages 135 and 144, there are extra columns for **-nce**, **-age** and **nge**, which are common endings.

While the pupil is learning these new letter-groups, play the previous games. You may wish to make one 'Is It?'

booklet for soft **c**, one for soft **g**, or six booklets, one for each letter-group.

This may be a good time to point out that printed material often shows: **a** as a, **g** as g.

Double c

When you have a **cc** before **a**, **o** or **u**, it says **k**: **accost, accord, accustom**.

When you have a **cc** before **e**, **i** or **y** (the letters that make **c** soft), the first says **k** and the second says **s**, so that **cc** sounds like **x**: **succeed, success, accept, accent, access, accelerate**. Note that **Dixon** and **Dickson** sound the same.

If you can notice the **-cess** in words, it helps to remember when you use **cc** and when **ss**: **access, success, princess, recess, abscess, necessary**.

Soft c

ce	ci	cy
fence	pencil	cylinder
dance	city	fancy
advance	accident	Nancy
success	decide	Cynthia
necessary	excited	Cyril
December	scissors	bicycle

So when do you use **c**, when **k**, and when **ck**?

ck, k, c

Ck follows a short vowel in words like **pack, peck, pick, rock, duck**.

The **ack, eck, ick** pattern is kept in **packet** (see page 105).

After a long vowel, the **k** sound is the hard 'kuh': **bake, like, stoke, duke, week, peak, steak**.

In a long word ending in the sound **ick**, it is spelt **ic**:

panic, **picnic**, **frantic**, **mimic**, **logic**, **magic**, **fantastic**, **Atlantic**, **Pacific**, **arithmetic**.

At the beginning of a word, the **k** sound before **a**, **o**, **u** appears as the letter **c**: **cat**, **cot**, **cut**; but before **e**, **i**, **y**, it is **k** (because **ce**, **ci**, **cy** have the **s** sound):

cat				sat
	kettle	centre		set
	kitten	city		sit
cot				
cut		cycle		

Point out to the child that he is learning how letters work together. Get him to think about the following and why they are spelt the way they are:

lack	lake	lace	lacking		lacing
lick	like	lice	licking	liking	
duck	duke		ducking		
trick	trike	trice	tricking		
prick		price	pricking		pricing
	make	mace		making	

Get the pupil to fill in the spaces and sound out the words.

ce	-ce	-nce
	after a long vowel	
centre	face	dance
ac____pt	spa____	gla____
ex____pt	gra____	adva____
ne____ssary	la____	Fra____
pro____ss	re____nt	dista____
ac____ss	de____nt	ambula____
suc____ss	twi____	arroga____
suc____ed	pri____	differe____
____ntury	mi____	lice____
____rtain	ri____	sente____
as____nd	o____an	prete____
des____nd	gro____r	mi____
for____	produ____r	wi____
____ment	redu____	pri____ss
con____al	noti____	insiste____
____nt	poli____	co____rt
s____nt	offi____	o____*

* once is an irregular word, linked to one.

Get the pupil to fill in the spaces and sound out the words.

ci	cy
city	fan**cy**
electri____ty	Nan____
ac____dent	chan____
pen____l	mer____
de____de	decen____
ex____ted	emergen____
____rcle	i____
____rcus	____st
____nema	C__ril
s____ssors	C__nthia
ra____ng	____anide
i____ng	____clone
medi____ne	____press (a tree)
____nders	bi____cle
in____dent	litera____
____trus	democra____
____der	lenien____

Soft g = j

ge	gi	gy
gentle	engine	gymnastics
fringe	magic	energy
sponge	tragic	allergy
village	digital	biology
bandage	imagine	zoology
manage	register	Egypt
cabbage	ginger	

My father's first name was George. All my life, until I learned the rule about **ge**, I wondered why his name had such an odd spelling. I learned this rule when I was 48! So you are way ahead of me!

In a word like **age**, **Regent**, **digest**, **(Stoke) Poges**, **huge**, the first vowel has an **e** two letters later, so the first vowel is long.

The same thing is found with **ce**; **face**, **recent**, **slicer**, **grocer**, **reduce** (**ace**, **ece**, **ice**, **oce**, **uce**).

If you want a short vowel in front of **ge**, instead of putting two **g's** (except in **suggest**, **exaggerate**) we put -**dge**:

badge	hedge	bridge	lodge	smudge

This is voiced. The unvoiced equivalent is **tch**:

patch	fetch	witch	Scotch	Dutch

So, surprisingly, it is the simple **rich**, **much**, **such**, **which**, **Duchess** that are irregular!

Words for Bingo

accept	ambulance	bicycle
chance	change	city
danger	December	decent
digital	excellent	except
face	fancy	manage
general	giant	ginger
grocer	hedge	hinge
huge	ice	imagine
necessary	police	princess
register	scarcely	sponge
suggest	village	

Note that the **ar** in **scarcely** does not sound as in **car**, but sounds like **air**. This is a very difficult word.

Many words end in **-nge**. When **-nge** follows **e, i, o, u,** the vowel is short (**hinge**), but **a** is different. In **orange**, the **a** sounds like **i**. In other words, the **a** is long:

range, ranger, change, danger, stranger, mange, manger, angel.

Many words end in **-age**. The word **age** has a long, clear **ay** sound. When the **-age** is an ending of a longer two-syllable word, we do not say it as a clear **age**. It sounds more like **-idge**. You could say each word first with a long **a** – vill-ay-j . . . vill-idge – if you wanted to: **village, cabbage, image, bandage, postage, manage.**

In **barrage** (like **camouflage, sabotage** and, in some regional speech, **garage**), we use more a French pronunciation: **ba'rrahj**.

Jokes (for dictation)
1. How do you start a teddy-bear race?
   Say, 'Ready . . . teddy . . . go!
2. 'Gary, did your sister help you with this exercise?'
   'No, miss. She did the lot.'

3. What's the difference between a bottle of medicine
    and a doormat?
    *One is shaken up and taken, and the other is taken up
    and shaken.*

Exercise
Get the pupil to write **ge** in the following words and say
the word. Then for the first twelve words, get him to find
the picture on the following pages and write the word
beside it.

ca__	brid__	cotta__
sled__	bad__	bad__r
bud__rigar	hin__	oran__s
pa__	__ms	banda__

an__l	dama__	a__
mana__	spon__	frin__
passa__	hu__	sur__on
fud__	wa__	gara__
G_or__	dun__on	jud__
sta__	villa__	__ntle
dan__r	lar__	ra__
cabba__	chan__	

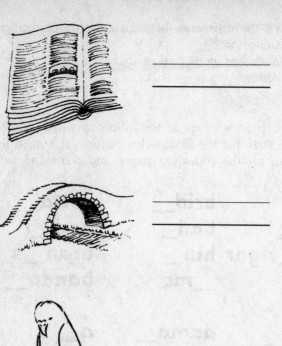

_____

_____

_____

_____

_____

_____

_____

_____

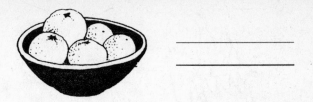

_____
_____

_____
_____

_____
_____

_____
_____

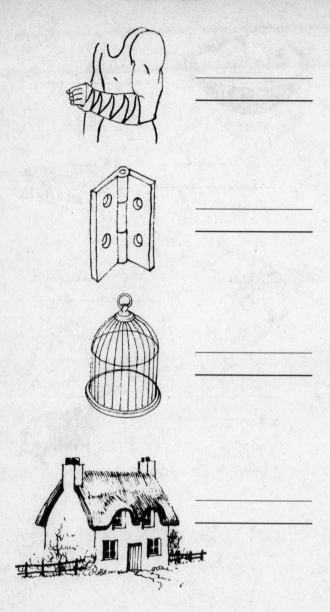

Get the child to do one column a day.

-tch	-dge
hatch	badge
scra___	e___
stre___	le___
wi___	he___
hi___	bri___
pi___	sto___
sti___	fu___
di___	ju___
Sco___	gru___
clu___	nu___
bu___er	slu___
Du___	bu___t

In words of more than one syllable, **-age** sounds like **-idge**.

ge	-nge	-age
gentle	fringe	rage

wa__	hi___	man___
lar__	plu___	vill___
ur__nt	spo___	dam___
G_or__	ora___	cabb___
Re__nt	cha__	band___
di__st	da___r	sav___
Ni__l	a___l	pass___
co__nt	stra___r	im___
hu__	ra__r	lugg___
sug__st		post___
exag__rate		

gi

magic

tra____c
ima____ne
____raffe
____nger
____ant
re____ster
en____ne
di____tal
a____tate
____gantic

gy

Egypt

____mnastics
aller____
biolo____
zoolo____
ornitholo____
sociolo____
gemmolo____
geolo____
criminolo____
bacteriolo____

gi, gy; ce, ci, cy

Copy the following. Get the pupil to fill the gaps then write the starred words beside the appropriate picture on the following pages.

gi

*__raffe	*en__ne	ima__ne
tra__c	__ant	ma__c
re__ster	di__tal	__nger

gy

*__mnastics	E__pt	zoolo__
ener__	aller__	biolo__

ce

fa__	*la__s	pri__
sli__	*pen__	di__
fen__	*s__nt	

-nce

da___	dista___	mi___r
*ambula___	pri___ss	Fra___
pri___	gla___	si___
adva___	differe___	

ci

*pen__l	*__rcle	electri__ty
ex__ted	ac__dent	de__de
__ty	s__ssors	__nema
__garette	pre__ous	

cy

*__linder	__clone	__gnet
C__ril	Nan__	bi__cle
fan__		

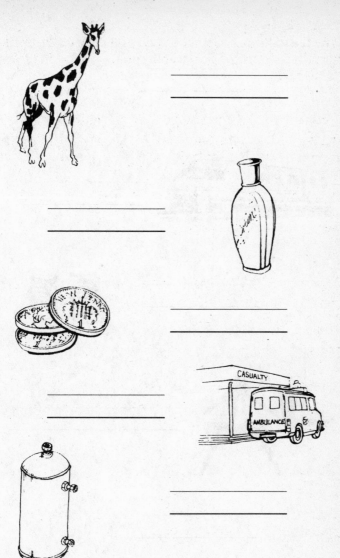

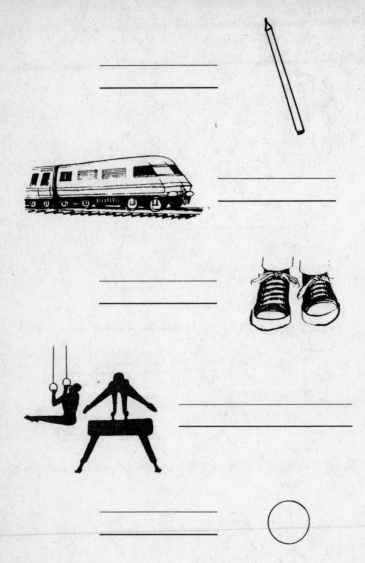

By now you may have started the pupil on reading books, or you have encouraged him gradually to read more and more of the words (that you know he can read) when you read together. When reading any books with large print, just help with words that have letter-groups not yet taught, or irregular words. Use your judgment.

STEP 69

gu

If **ge**, **gi**, **gy** say **je**, **ji**, **jy**, what if we do not want this? If we want a hard **g** in front of **e**, **i**, **y**, we must split the **ge**, **gi**, **gy**, and we do this with a **u**: **gu** says the hard **g**. It forms a 'wall' between the **g** and the **e**, **i**, **y**.

There is a **u** in **guard**, a **u** which is not really needed. Compare it with **regard**. Note also that the West Indian island **Antigua** is pronounced **Antee-ga**, not **Antig-ew-a**.

gu
guitar
_____**ess**
_____**est**
_____**ide**
_____**ilty**
_____**illotine**
_____**inea pig**
G_____**y**
_____**ard** (but **regard**)

STEPS 70 AND 71

ou

The next letter-groups to learn are based on the following rule: No English word ends in **u**.

Menu is French. **You** is the exception.

As with **i/y**, we can put **a** and **o** in front of **u/w**. If **u** would be at the end, we change it to a **w**. **Ou** can make at least five sounds, **ow** two, but **au/aw** are totally consistent and make only one sound. It is surprising, therefore, that of all these sounds and spellings, it is **au** that usually takes longest to learn.

ou

ou (silent **o**)

$8 \times 2 = 16$

cl____d
sh____t
gr____nd
s____th
c____nt
tr____sers

d____ble
n____rish
c____ntry
c____sin
curi____s

-our sounds like **or**: **pour**, **four**.

    -ou can say **oo**: **you**, **youth**, **group**, **soup**, **coupon**, **route**, **routine**.

    -ou also changes its sound in the **ough** words, see page 161.

    -ou says short **u** in **-ous**: **famous**, **curious**, **precious**, **spacious**, **delicious**, **avaricious**.

STEPS 72 AND 73

ow

If we want the **ou** sound in **cloud** at the end, we must change **ou** to **ow**: but **ow** can say two sounds:

ow	ow
____l	b____l
c____	sn____
t____n	gr____
cr____n	thr____
cr____d	pill____
p____der	borr____
h____, n____	yell____

Get the pupil to find pictures for these words on the two next pages:

cow, house, mower, elbow, flower, mouse, pillow, cloud, towel, shower.

ou/ow

_____

_____

ou/ow

Get the pupil to fill in the gaps and say the words.

ou	ou	ow	ow
ou t	y ou ng	c ow	sn ow
sh__t	d__ble	__l	gr__
ab__t	tr__ble	t__n	sh__
gr__nd	c__ple	d__n	thr__
s__nd	c__ntry	dr__n	m__er
p__nd	c__sin	p__der	pill__
s__th	n__rish	sh__er	yell__
m__th	enc__rage	fl__er	sorr__
h__se	furi__s	cr__d	bl__
m__se	fam__s	t__el	arr__
tr__sers	delici__s	cl__n	fl__
c__nt	feroci__s	t__er	borr__

au aw

These two letter-groups say the same sound and are very reliable.

au

aw

au	aw
P____l	s____
A___gust	p____
h____nted	cl____
bec____se	l____n
l____ndry	y____n
____tomatic	str____
l____nch	outl____
s____ce	cr____l

Jokes (for dictation)

1. Teacher: What was the first thing James I did on
                coming to the throne?
   Pupil: He sat down, miss.
2. Art Master: Billy, I told the class to draw a horse and
                cart, but you have only drawn the horse.
   Billy: Yes, sir. The horse will draw the cart.
3. Why do cows wear bells? *Their horns don't work.*
4. Why did the butterfly flutter by? *Because the dragon-
   fly drank the flagon dry.*

gh ght

Our beautiful language is made up of words from many other languages. When the Vikings came over, their language contained a sound in the back of the throat, a guttural that the Anglo-Saxons could not pronounce, so they got round it, either by leaving out the **gh** (as in **light**) or by putting in another sound, and they did not even keep to one sound! In **-ght** words (and others) the **g..h..** has Gone Home:

light	n_____	fr_____
s_____	t_____	m_____
f_____	fl_____	r_____
br_____		

Note: **sigh, high; eight, weight; weigh, neigh, neighbour, sleigh; deign, reign.** (See Step 99.)

Note also that here **ei** sounds as a long **a**.

STEP 78

ought

Ought sounds the same as **aught**:

ought, bought, brought, fought, thought, nought;

caught, taught, daughter, slaughter.

But: **laugh, laughter.**

STEPS 79-88

-ough

You have had **ou** and **gh**. Now we put them together. We cannot say, as we have done previously, '**ough** says . . .' because it says six different things, in addition to the way it sounds in the **ought** words.

This is the group of words from which people choose when they want to prove that phonics does not work. Well over 90% of English words are spelt regularly. Phonics accepts that the **-ough** words are a problem, but draws attention, as far as possible, to the regularities within them; for example, the **thr** in **through** and the **r** in **rough**. When pupils are fluent in regular words, they usually take exceptions in their stride.

In	**cough**	}	the **ough**
	trough	}	says **off**
In	**enough**	}	the **ough**
	r_____	}	says **uff**
	t_____	}	
In	**pl_____**	}	the **ough**
	b_____	}	says **ow** as in **cow**

In	**thr**_____		the **ough**
	(one word only)		says **oo**

In	**d**_____	}	the **ough**
	alth_____	}	says **Oh!**, the long sound of the vowel **o**

In	**thor**_____**ly**	}	the **ough**
	bor_____	}	says **u** as in **cup**
	Scarbor_____	}	

In	**Loughborough**	the first **ough** says **uff** and the second a short **u** **Luffburru**

Get the child to read down the words, first with the help of pronunciation clues, then without, from top to bottom, then bottom to top, then at random. Then see if the child can spell them from dictation.

Copy the following in large-size letters onto a piece of paper and get the child to fill in the gaps with words containing **-ough** from the list above:

1. **Billy ____ed all _____ the night; he could not get _____ sleep,_____ he did take his medicine.**

2. **The pig ate from a _____ under the _____ of a tree. The farmer _____ed his field _____ly.**

3. **The _____ was in an inner city, with a lot of _____, _____ boys.**

4. **The baker mixed _____ before he made bread.**

(Answers: coughed, through, enough, although, trough, bough, ploughed, thoroughly, borough, rough, tough, dough)

From this point, you will probably not need more games. It is enough just to do the writing and practise the lists of words. You can play games from previous Steps as a form of revision. Remind the child of the rules of each game before he begins.

STEP 89

wa

Wa hardly ever says the sound in **wax**, **waggle**. It sounds like **wo**. **Qua** (except in **quack**) sounds like **kwo**; **quar** sounds like **kwor**. **War** sounds like **wor**, and **wor** sounds like **wer**. By now, just completing the words in a column (pronounce correctly, know what it means, or ask) is sufficient to deal with the remaining letter-groups. Continue to play the old games. Read through one early letter-group word list each day.

wa	war	qua	quar
__s	__m	__rrel	___t
__nt	__ning	__rry	___ter
__sh	__den	__lity	___tz
__tch	s__m	__ntity	
__sp	re__d	s__sh	
__ffle	back__d	s__bble	
__nd	for__ds	s__dron	
s__n	to__ds	__rantine	
s__llow	a__d		
_h_t			

STEP 90

wh and short words

Question words begin with **wh**, and the **h** is sounded, and not silent: **what, when, who, which, where, why, whether, whither**.

Who is an irregular word.

In short words, some vowels say their long sound:

my	fly	cry	why
try	fry	shy	spy
dry	sky	guy	

or say their name:

sold	bold	gold	c_____
f_____	h_____	t_____	w_____

so	no	go	fro
Lo!			

(**to, who** and **do** are exceptions)

he	we	be	me

STEP 91

al wor

In a few words, **al** says **aw**. Copy the following and get the pupil to write **al** in the gaps:

all, ball, c__l, t__l, st__l, sm__l, h__l, f__l, w__l, __der, w__k, t__k, ch__k, st__k, F__klands, h__t, m__t, s__t, b__d, sc__d, __so, __most, __ways, __together, __though.

Wor says **wer**. Again, get the pupil to fill in the gaps:
___d, ___ld, ___m, ___k, ___th, ___se, ___st.

Joke
If mud makes bricks and bricks make walls, what do walls make? *Ice-cream!*
[In the UK, Walls is a company making ice-cream.]

Exercise
Get the pupil to find the pictures for these words on the following pages:
straw, lawn, paw, ball, draw, gauntlet, sauce, wall.

au, aw; al

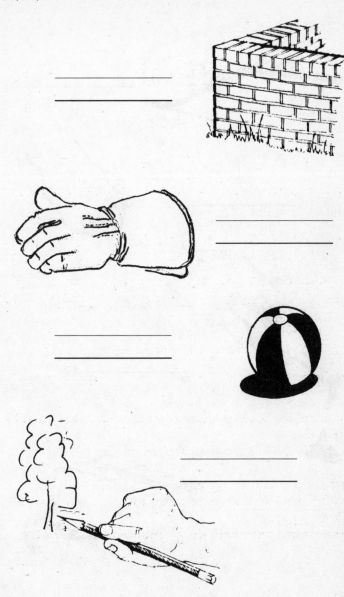

au, aw; al

_____

_____

_____

_____

_____

_____

_____

_____

Words of French origin

In words that come from French, **i** sounds like **ee** (**-ine**, **-igue**, **-ique**); **ch** = **sh**; endings **-que** and **-gue** sound like **k** and hard **g**.

-ine

machine	Paul_____	tanger_____
guillot_____	magaz_____	margar_____
nectar_____	mar_____	trampol_____

ch

chef	ma____ine

-que

anti_____	uni_____	grotes_____
che_____	pictures_____	

-gue

catalo_____	va_____	lea_____
intri_____	fati_____	ro_____
dialo_____	vo_____	

STEP 93

The long sound of **u**

The pupil has already learned the first two ways of spelling the long sound of **u**, as in **valUE**, **cUbE**, using **ue** and **u-e** (magic **e**). The third column of words is similar, showing that *any* vowel two letters after a **u** can make the **u** say its name. The fourth column is **ui**, with only about half a dozen words, and finally **ew**. To remember **blew** from **blue**, make the connection with the **w** (**ow**, **ew**), that **blow** and **blew** go together, also **grow**, **grew**; **throw**, **threw** (not **through**).

ue	u-e	-u-	ui	ew
blue	cube	music	suit	new
cl__	t_b_	p_pil	fr__t	f__
gl__	t_n_	_niform	recr__t	st__
c__	f_m_s	_nion	purs__t	gr__ *(grow)*
val__	c_r_	t_lip	j__ce	thr__ *(throw)*
tiss__	ac_t_	h_mid	br__se	bl__ *(blow)*
stat__	st_d_nt	_s_al	cr__se	fl__ *(fly)*
resc__	_s_	c_pid	purs__t	scr__
aven__	am_s_	pec_liar		st__ard
que__	exc_s_	st_pid		vi__
purs__	comp_t_r	d_ty		revi__
d__	d_k_	_niversity		p___

STEP 94

Words of Greek origin

Another language from which we get many words is Greek. In these words, **ph** says **f** and **ch** says **k**.

ph

dolphin, ele__ant, or__an, P_ilip, ne__ew, tele__one, al__abet, __otogra__, __antom, __easant

ch

school, e__o, __emist, an__or, C_ristmas, __orus, Ni__olas, __aracter, stoma__-a__e

Exercise

Get the pupil to say these words, then write them beside the right picture on the following pages:

ph says f in these words: **dolphin, elephant, telephone**

wa says wo in these words: **watch, waffle, swan, swallow, wasp**

-ine says -een at the end of words: **trampoline, magazine, margarine, guillotine.**

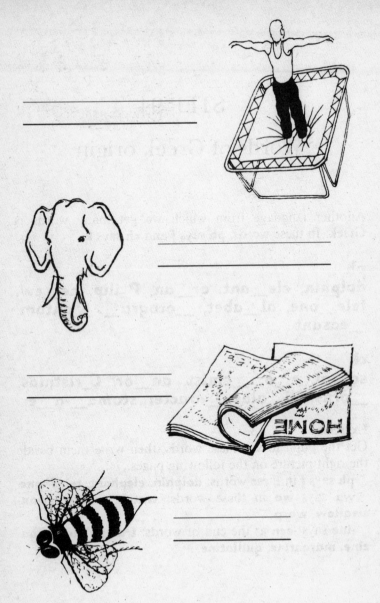

_____
_____

_____
_____

_____
_____

_____
_____

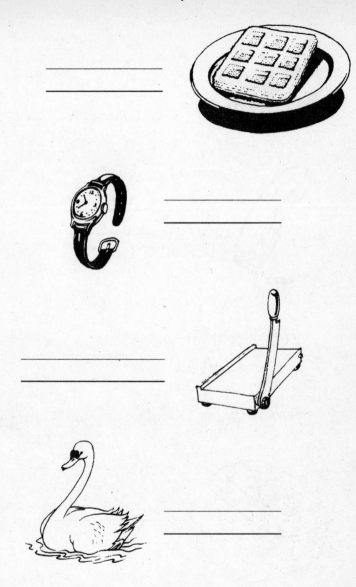

_____

_____

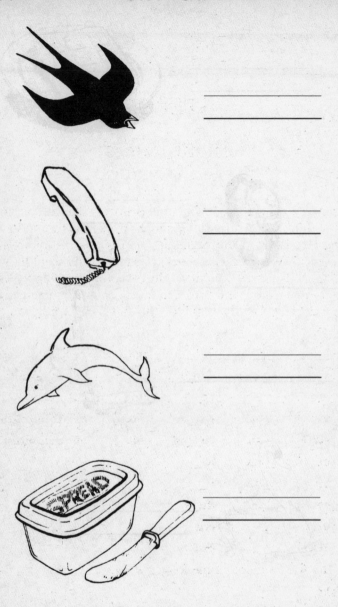

_____
_____

_____
_____

_____
_____

_____
_____

STEP 95

Silent letters

Some letters are silent, but this is not as difficult as you may think, because initial **k** and **g** go silent before **n**. **W** is silent before **r** at the beginning, and in two words in the middle (**Norwich** and **answer**). There is also a silent **b** or **n** at the end after **m**. The silent **l** in **yolk**, **folk**, only applies in those two words, and before **m** in **psalm**, **palm**, **calm**, and in **half**, **calf**. Get the pupil to write out these words two or three times.

kn_	wr_	-mb	-mn	
knife	wrong	climb	hymn	but hymnal*
__ight	__ist	co__	autu__	but autumnal*
__ow	__eck	cli__ed	sole__	but solemnity*
__ew	__en	co__ed	colu__	but columnar*
__ot	__ap	la__		
__ob	__ite	li__		
__ee	__ing	du__		
__ock		cru__		
__uckle		thu__		

* **The n** is sounded in the longer word.

Joke
What lies at the bottom of the sea and shivers? *A nervous wreck!*

STEP 96

Silent **h**, **g**

hour	**_onest**	**_onour**	**g_ost**
gnash	**_nat**	**_naw**	**_nome**	**_nu** *(an animal)*

Sign but **signal**, **signature**: sound the **g** in the longer words.

Make sure that the pupil knows the meaning of these words. Some of them are likely to be new words.

Joke (for dictation)
'How do you spell "wrong"?'
'R..o..n..g.'
'That's wrong.'
'That's what you asked for, wasn't it?'

STEP 97

-tion

In a very few words, **ti** says **sh** which is very strange. In many, many words, **on** says **un**; it hardly ever says the sound in **on**, except in words beginning with **con-**. If you put **ti** before **on**, you have **-tion** which is a common ending and sounds like 'shun'. (The exception is **question**, sounded as **questi..on**.) In these words, the stress is on the syllable before the -tion. There are hundreds of words like this. Many words end in **ation**, and in these words the **a** is long and has the stress. 'Stress' means more emphasis on the syllable, spoken on a higher note than the other syllables.

ti = sh	on = un	-tion = shun	-ation
patient	won	suction	station
cau__ous	s__	ac____	sens____
ini__al	d__e	men____	decor____
essen__al	fr__t	atten____	inform___
confiden__al	__i__	inven____	educ____
influen__al	L__d__	inspec____	consider__
iner__a	pers__	prescrip__	ventil____
pruden__al	m__th	addi____	popul____
	ribb__	subtrac___	separ____
	cart__	por____	associ____

177

When the root word ends in **-it**, 'shun' is spelt **-ssion**:

omit	omission
emit	emission
permit	permission
admit	admission

When the root word ends in **-ess** or **-uss**, the **-ss** is kept in the ending:

impress	impression
process	procession
access	accession
success	succession *(to the throne)*
express	expression
depress	depression
confess	confession
concuss	concussion

In the **-sion** ending, the **s** sounds like **z**: **television**. Note that the only words where a **shun** ending is spelt **sh** are **cushion** and **fashion**.

STEP 98

-ture

Another common ending is **-ture**, which we would expect to rhyme with **endure**, but it says **cher**, like a short sneeze.

Capture sounds like **captsha** or **capcher**. Get the pupil to complete the following words with **-ture**:

adven_____   furni_____   pic_____
punc_____   fix_____   scrip_____
mix_____   lec_____

When the first syllable ends in a vowel, its vowel is long:

fu_____   na_____   crea_____

STEP 99

ie

Ie usually says the long **i** sound: **pie**, **tie**, **cried**. It can say **ee** in:

field	chief		priest
yield	grief	grieve	piece*
shield	relief	relieve	
	belief	believe	
	thief	thieve	

* Say **A piece of pie**.

There is a rule, '**i** before **e**, except after **c**' (as in **ceiling, receive, deceive, conceit, receipt**) but there are as many exceptions as regular words: **their, leisure, seize, neither, foreign**, and a few more. **Ei** sometimes says **ay**: **vein, veil, reign, eight, weight, weigh, neigh, sleigh, neighbour, reindeer**. Note **eir** in **their**.

STEP 100

be- re- de-

Many words begin with **be-**, **re-**, **de-**. If you get used to this, you will sound out **begin** correctly and not be put off by sounding **beg . . .in**.

<u>be</u>gin	<u>re</u>fresh	<u>de</u>cay
__hind	__mind	__lay
__come	__fuse	__fy
__cause	__gret	__fend
__long	__member	__sire
__have*	__alise	__pend
__lieve	__sult	__clare

and many more

(* long **a**)

181

Finally

Now, how long did the whole programme take? Check the
date you started. By now, the pupil will be a good reader.
There are still rules to learn, but for most people this
foundation is more than enough. Over 90% of words are
regularly spelt. This programme does not cover irregular
words, but even irregular words have some letters that are
regular, that 'work'.

If the new reader can now have plenty of books, choos-
ing them from the local library, large-print at first, and
reading is made an activity enjoyed by all the family, you
will have given your pupil a lifetime of pleasure and, I
hope, enjoyed doing so.

GAMES

Pairs

You need a set of 52 blank playing cards or similar sized cards. Look through mail order catalogues and magazines and cut out pairs of pictures of three-lettered objects. You will need two sets of 13 pictures, making 26 in total. Stick each picture onto one of the cards. Then write the name of each object onto two cards, thereby using the remaining 26 cards.

Put all the cards out face-down. A player turns up one card, then a second: if they are a pair (either two words or two pictures, or word and picture, of the same object) that player has another turn. If the cards are not a pair, someone else has a turn. If the pupil finds it difficult playing with 52 cards, start with only half the cards, but be sure you play with full sets of four cards for each word.

Bingo

Three-letter word bingo can be played with two or more players once all the letters of the alphabet have been taught (Step 26). For each Bingo game, I use 32 words. Each player needs a card 13cm × 15cm (5" × 6") displaying 16 of the words in four rows. See the grid overleaf. Each of the 32 words also needs to be written on a separate small card. If only two people play, they can use the individual word-cards to 'cover up', but if more than two play, each player needs 16 small, blank cover-up cards. I cut these from an

sun	lid	red	run
fix	rod	wig	van
lot	get	cat	tap
sit	men	let	jug

Example bingo grid

old tissue box, and the pupil can then use them for all future Bingo games.

The individual word-cards are placed in a pile. The players take it in turns to take a card from the pile and read out the word. The player who has that word on his larger card, takes the small card to cover up that word on his larger card. I turn them over, so that, as play proceeds, words disappear and you can only see the words you need. When a player has a line, he shouts, 'Bingo!', and gets a *small* prize (raisin, sweet, etc).

A line can be either horizontal (across), vertical (down) or diagonal (from corner to corner); use these long words and explain them! Expand the child's vocabulary all the time. I usually keep playing until there have been five wins per card: line, line, line, 'round the outside' (12 words) and a full card.

Some of the words I use at the end of Step 26 are shown in the grid opposite. The other 16 words I use are: **ran, bag, wet, set, zip, win, hot, fox, cup, dog, man, rag, wax, hit, ten, gun**.

'Is it?' books

Place a blank A4 piece of paper portrait way up. Fold it in three horizontally and cut across the folds. Repeat with another piece of paper so that you have six sheets of paper lying on top of each other horizontally. Fold them in half vertically and staple or sellotape along the fold, making a small booklet. Write a three-letter word on one side, and stick or draw a picture matching that word on the back, the other side. The pupil cannot see the picture until he has read the word, and turns over merely to confirm that he did get the word right.

The Dice Game

This is a board game like snakes-and-ladders. See the example on pages 186 and 187. Making this by cutting out pictures from magazines and mail order catalogues can be

Start	Run on six	Go on to a net	
			Run on to a dog
Run on to a bib	Run on to a web		Go on to a cot
	Run on six	Go back to a can	Go on to a gun
Go on to a gun			

Run on to a ten	Go to a bag	**10**	
			Go back to a ten
Go on to a doll		Go back to a web	Go on to a can
	Go back to a gun		WIN

a happy family activity. Remember at the beginning you can only use simple three-letter words, not **saw**, **car**, **eye**, where there is not one simple sound per letter. I make the first letter in any square a capital thereby introducing capitals to the pupil. The first square after *Start* I usually make 'Run on six' to turn a slow start into a good start.

Vowel Puzzles
Make a 3 × 3 grid. Write a selection of different consonants in the spaces around the outside. Then, in a different colour, write a vowel in the centre space. Get the pupil to make up as many three-letter words as he can using the consonants and that one vowel.

c	f	p
m	**a**	t
d	g	n

From the above grid, the pupil could find: **cat**, **can**, **fat**, **fan**, **pat**, **pan**, **mat**, **man**, **dam**, **gap**, **tap**, **tan**, etc.

Once the pupil has progressed further, you can adapt the grid to feature different letter-groups: instead of putting a vowel in the centre square, put a letter-group like **ou**. Then write other letters or letter-groups in the outside squares, as in the following example:

c	r	pr
cl	**ou**	nt
f	d	nd

d	h	m	p	u	z
c	h	l	d	t	ʄ
c	g	l	d	t	ʄ
c	g	l	o	s	x
b	f	k	o	s	x
b	f	k	o	s	w
b	e	j	n	r	v
a	e	j	u	r	v
a	e	i	m	q	v
a	d	i	m	q	u

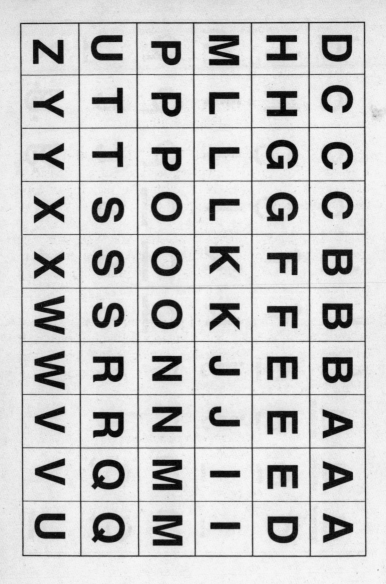

Z	U	P	M	H	D
Y	U	P	L	H	C
Y	T	P	L	G	C
X	S	P	L	G	C
X	S	O	L	G	C
X	S	O	K	F	B
W	S	O	K	F	B
W	R	O	J	E	B
V	R	N	J	E	A
V	R	N	J	E	A
V	Q	M	I	E	A
U	Q	M	I	D	A

RIGHT WAY
PUBLISHING POLICY

HOW WE SELECT TITLES

RIGHT WAY consider carefully every deserving manuscript. Where an author is an authority on his subject but an inexperienced writer, we provide first-class editorial help. The standards we set make sure that every **RIGHT WAY** book is practical, easy to understand, concise, informative and delightful to read. Our specialist artists are skilled at creating simple illustrations which augment the text wherever necessary.

CONSISTENT QUALITY

At every reprint our books are updated where appropriate, giving our authors the opportunity to include new information.

FAST DELIVERY

We sell **RIGHT WAY** books to the best bookshops throughout the world. It may be that your bookseller has run out of stock of a particular title. If so, he can order more from us at any time – we have a fine reputation for "same day" despatch, and we supply any order, however small (even a single copy), to any bookseller who has an account with us. We prefer you to buy from your bookseller, as this reminds him of the strong underlying public demand for **RIGHT WAY** books. However, you can order direct from us by post, by phone with a credit card, or through our web site.

FREE

If you would like an up-to-date list of all **RIGHT WAY** titles currently available, please send a stamped self-addressed envelope to

ELLIOT RIGHT WAY BOOKS, BRIGHTON ROAD, LOWER KINGSWOOD, TADWORTH, SURREY, KT20 6TD, U.K.
or visit our web site at www.right-way.co.uk